Elam Rush Stimson

History of the Separation of Church and State in Canada

Second Edition

Elam Rush Stimson

History of the Separation of Church and State in Canada
Second Edition

ISBN/EAN: 9783337190415

Printed in Europe, USA, Canada, Australia, Japan

Cover: Foto ©ninafisch / pixelio.de

More available books at **www.hansebooks.com**

HISTORY OF THE SEPARATION

OF

CHURCH AND STATE

IN CANADA.

EDITED BY

THE REV. E. R. STIMSON, M.A.

SECOND EDITION.

Toronto.

1887.

ENTERED, according to the Act of the Parliament of Canada, in the year one thousand eight hundred and eighty-seven, by the Reverend ELAM RUSH STIMSON, M.A., in the Office of the Minister of Agriculture at Ottawa.

DEDICATION.

THE EDITOR unites gratitude with cheerful acknowledgments in dedicating this compilation to his PATRONS.

The sympathy they have given to him under a deprivation which neither wisdom commends nor Christianity sustains is as consolatory as a restoration of the means of subsistence which a sentiment of generosity induced him to bestow for the "maintenance and support" of successors in the ministry *after*, not *before*, his death.

78 BEVERLEY STREET,
TORONTO, CANADA,
January 1st, 1887.

CONTENTS.

CHAPTER I.

Early Days—Memories—Church and State Doctrines—Application—Denominations 9

CHAPTER II.

Origin of Church and State (?) in Canada—King George III.—Clerics—See of Bath and Wells—Address to William Pitt—1791—Re-educating—Flexibility of New Countries 15

CHAPTER III.

Precedence—Loyalty—Loyalty of the Baptists 23

CHAPTER IV.

The Act of 1791—The "Protestant Clergy"—The Imperial Act of 1840—The Episcopal Church well cared for—But not satisfied—The question re-opened—Baptists in the field 27

CHAPTER V.

Methodist Influence—Patriotism—Rev. Wm. Ryerson's Speech—Rev. Dr. Ryerson's Memorandum on the Clergy Reserve Question—Settlement with the Methodists—The Amount of Money the Methodist Clergy might have had but did not take 44

CHAPTER VI.

Clergy Reserve Controversies in Canada, 1817-1831—Original Grant of Lands in 1791 for the Support of a Protestant Clergy—Proposal to Alienate them made in 1817—Episcopal Clergy Corporations Established—Exclusive Claims of Clergy of Church of England—Petition of Dr. Strachan, as Chairman of Clergy Corporation, in 1823, and appended Ecclesiastical Chart—Action of Legislative Assembly in 1825-1826—Grant of £750 to Scottish Clergy—King's College Charter: its Sectarian Character—Dr. Strachan's Letter and Ecclesiastical Chart of 1827—Investigation by Committee of Imperial House of Commons—Letters of Bishop of Quebec and of Scottish Clergy on the Clergy Reserves in 1827-1828—Claims of Clergy of the United Presbytery of Upper Canada—Ultimate Disposal of the Clergy Reserves 83

CONTENTS. vii

CHAPTER VII.

Catholicism in London—Early Settlers—Early Difficulties—Progress and Voluntaryism—Quiet Patriotism—Correspondence 149

CHAPTER VIII.

Early Excitement—Imperial Legislation—Existing Interests Guaranteed—A Protest—Canadian Legislation and Protection—Bishop Strachan—The Clergy Influenced—The Hon. J. H. Cameron—Table Showing who Commuted—Blending of Church and State. 159

CHAPTER IX.

Accessions of Capital to Diocese of Huron—Agreement with the Clergy—Disputed—Generosity of Clergy Acknowledged—Address to the Hon. J. H. Cameron—Popular Suppositions—Speech of Rev. Benjamin Cronyn—Reply of Rev. J. Winterbotham—Speech of Rev. Wm. Ryerson—Centralization—Clerical Visits and Grand Expectations—Exceptions Taken and Predictions—Influences of Endowments—Truths Circulated in England 183

CONCLUSION.

Beauties of Government—Light-hearted Ignorance—A Popular Mistake—Clergy Reserve Money belongs to all without reference to Race or Denomination .... PAGE 196

Separation of Church and State.

CHAPTER I.

Early Days—Memories—Church and State Doctrines—
Application—Denominations.

THE early days of Canada were exciting ones. The first inhabitants, not aborigines, possessed a vigour and ingenuity of character absent from the material training and social discipline of emigrants, and they became a nucleus around which others were to settle.

The first stock will naturally and forever possess a sense of primal constructiveness. So it has been and is with every colony. Mutual dependence, and the title acquired for mutual advantages, are qualities which inspire the thoughtful and industrious with no mean aspirations, and with a disrelish for the assumptions of strangers, which too often produce neither happiness nor prosperity.

We know such ideas are in conflict with the attitude taken by the Crown during the close of the last century, nor do they harmonize with much of the leaven which landed upon our shores during the first half of this century. We have, though, no desire to perpetuate the conflict nor induce the opposition of such people as we are glad to welcome.

Our desire is to refresh the memories of those who are younger than ourselves in the country, and to participate in instructive correspondence with those who are older; to perpetuate a record of large principles asserted by the State with parental solicitude, and of counter ones by a great many people at a period when the plastic hand of settlement directed us to exactly what we are as a Dominion.

Such thoughts gather encouragement from the large histories upon different subjects connected with Canada lately given by the pens of authors of the first merit. Their histories have become acknowledged in a general reception by the public; and we hope that, as they have proved to be acceptable, so this compilation will meet with favour, and the editor escape from an equivocal observation, of which he will entertain enduring recollections.

Church and State as a political doctrine was taught for the purpose of assisting the poor in a poor new country, and carrying the principles of Christianity to every man's door. There being now about four millions of dollars held as Trust Funds within the limits of old Upper Canada, it is not a censurable question to ask to what extent did each individual profit, say, about the time of the Rebellion of 1837-8, and now, when it is supposed that Church and State is a connection or condition totally eradicated from civic control—what advantage is derivable, say, to each individual in the provincial city of London?

During early days the question obtained an answer in the civil strife it promoted, in the personal animosities it fanned into exercise, and the scandal relatives and neighbours uttered against each other according to the shades of interest they took in it. And for the last ten years, in the western part of Western Canada especially, all the characteristics of early contention have been burning under the surface, only perhaps with more rancour and power of ruining individuals than when the State was an almoner of Church endowments.

When Church and State first took effect in what is now the city of London there were eight or ten Methodists, no Baptists, no Congregationalists, a few Presbyterians, and a few Roman Catholics, with a remainder of the population as members of the Church of England. It would be invidious to enumerate the numbers of different denominations now, how they have attained to such numbers, to contrast the magnificence of their voluntary Church properties and the superior position they all occupy.

Suspending such remembrances for the present, a reflection presents itself in the circumstance that, as children love to mark their height upon the wall to see how much they have grown from time to time, so every one is interested in the growth of Christian denominations to see whether their grains of mustard seed, sown in weakness, have been raised with beneficent shadows and are productive of the fruit they promised. The moral is found in Tennyson's Yorkshire farmer; but who so laggard as to transport that farmer to Canada? The citizen sufficiently spiritless will hardly hold rank with volunteers, and charitably we will protect him from going to the tomb unsung and unhonoured. Inquiries are abroad, and to be without answers is an affirmation of what is almost a "saw": " If ignorance is bliss, 'tis folly to be wise."

At first in our history the view was comprehensive enough to assert a general citizenship and a like general claim to profits arising from territory known as "Crown Lands." Intelligence so large includes respect for all Christians. If precedent and history are advanced in their favour, let them be credited. If usefulness and moral worth distinguish them as a family, by all means accord an approval. By no means live upon negations, as is the practice of some; and in the end we will see whether pleasure and profit are not fruit largely gathered from gardens hedged and watered by our neighbours.

CHAPTER II.

Origin of Church and State in Canada (?)—King George III.—Clerics—See of Bath and Wells—Address to William Pitt—1791—Re-educating—Flexibility of New Countries.

ROM an early period in England, as well as other countries on the Continent, the principle has been received and acted upon that the Government is responsible for the religious sentiments of its subjects. But against this principle a contention has been waged for a great many years, both in Britain and, successfully, on the western side of the Atlantic ocean. Romance and stern reality have combined during the contention to produce scenes of fortitude and love for early practices and "first principles" not to be found described on the pages of romantic history, nor in the common records of our country.

As an instance of the truth of this, we have only to go to the writings of Mr. Leighton, who "was severely whipped; then, being set in the pillory, his ear was cut off, his nose slit, and his cheek was branded with a red-hot iron S. S., as a Sower of Sedition. On that day week—the sores on his back, ears, nose, and face not being cured—he was whipped again at the pillory in Cheapside, and the remainder of his sentence executed by cutting off his other ear, slitting the other side of his nose, and branding his other cheek."

When Canada was ceded to Great Britain, the principle of Church polity running concurrent with civil jurisdiction was confirmed. It was maintained with more or less vigour as circumstances favoured its adoption in all the colonies of the Western world, and culminated with their loss to the Empire after seven years of unprecedented conflict. King George III., yet smarting under the loss, anticipated the removal of causes for a separation of Church and State by making a grant of one-seventh of the territory of Upper Canada, for the "support and maintenance of a Protestant clergy," who, by a system of education compatible with loyalty to the Crown, might forever exterminate the idea of loyalty and piety being twin-sisters in the development of resources to be found in a new country. No sentiment is more potential than that of religion in the well-being of a State, and clerics are its special promoters. In the protection of Upper Canada, accordingly, the education they impart was sought to be encouraged by a grant of land adequate in value to the object anticipated. The word *clergie* is in itself historical, meaning in the Norman tongue, *literature*. In early times, when learning was almost exclusively with the clergy, they, by this monopoly, held almost the whole power of Church and State.

We may see an illustration of this union of civil and ecclesiastical functions in the Annals of the See of Bath and Wells, which yielded from its diocesan list to the civil state of England six Lord Chancellors, eight Lord High Treasurers, two Lords Privy Seal, one Master of the Rolls, one Lord President of Wales, one Principal Secretary of State; and to higher Episcopal office, four Archbishops of Canterbury, three Archbishops of York, and, says the annalist of the diocese, " to the Protestant Episcopal Church, the cause of Monarchy and of Orthodoxy, one MARTYR, William Laud."

As strong a front as such a record presents in favour of Church and State, it was ineffectual in perpetuating it in America. Its tendency in George the III.'s time was to expel the popular element of voluntaryism in the Old Country, and to give it growth along the eastern shores of the Western hemisphere. The British flag was waving over the ramparts of Louisburg, Niagara, Ticonderoga, Crown Point, Quebec, and all Canada; and an address presented to the celebrated William Pitt by the City of London, says: "Mr. Pitt left the thirteen British Colonies in North America in perfect security and happiness, every inhabitant then glowing with the warmest affection to the parent country. At home all was animation and industry. Riches and glory flowed in from every quarter." But the polity of Church and State embodied tainted principles of administration for those educated under a colonial regime, and, sniffing afar off in every breeze a spirit opposed to local government, and the recognition of tax-paying subjects themselves electing the objects to be paid for out of the public exchequer, a protest from every man's door was uttered against the adoption of a rule making the State the guardian of the religious convictions of the people. The result is well known. Religious Church education was sought to countervail it all, and the Clergy Reserves in 1791 were to constitute the capital for the monopoly of an education unacceptable to every one not a member of the Church of England.

Under the circumstances of the times, such an adoption can scarcely be reprobated. The very world itself was in a transitional condition as to modes of life, education, means of subsistence, and territorial occupation. Geographical experience had not given expansion to the minds of those whose vision compassed the limits of a small island; nor had enterprise opened the gates of a commerce hitherto unknown; nor had the education congenital with an existence among ourselves displayed to England that the ingenuity and habits of the young in a new country are the ones to give stability and patriotism to that country in manhood. That none other than the Church of England could furnish the State with *reliable* citizens was the impelling sentiment, and from this arose the union of Church and State (if the union ever existed) in Canada, and its subsidy of one-seventh of the provincial territory.

It took many years to uneducate England (if we may be permitted to use the word), and to incite her to the adoption of a colonial system of education and government calculated alike to confer upon her laurels of wealth, coherency and expansion.

No adverse reflection, however, should arise in the minds of the present or any other generation when reviewing the motives and temper of Great Britain between the years of 1791 and 1854-55—a period of time covering "Reserve" electoral excitement ; for it is to be remembered that the mother country is not as flexible in the acquisition of varied talents, nor as ready to apply them when acquired, as a youthful population who shape and organize the education and policy of a newly constituted colony. Besides, intercommunication was more difficult and less frequent in those days than at present, and many months were required to obtain a knowledge of public opinion even upon the spot. The wonder is that we are succeeding as well as we are, when it is observed that the leaven of some of our public institutions hankers for governing men who have had no education, no experience in the atmosphere of their labours.

The most successful scholastic establishments of 1886 are those of executive abilities and excellent mental training, acquired either by birth or many years of residence within the limits of the Dominion. An early opportunity may fortunately occur for showing that the retarding influences hinted at follow along and actuate with an unconscious impulse the conduct of the children born here, but having the parentage of the old-fashioned sons of Church and State. Their status is determined by accidental advantages, not meritorious wisdom. And the sooner they are superseded by intelligence based upon other metal, the more active will be the administration of equity and enterprise in the community where their influence is employed.

CHAPTER III.

Precedence—Loyalty—Loyalty of the Baptists.

WHO effected the separation of Church and State (if it ever existed) in Canada? This question is put as to individuals, and is too difficult to answer at once. It requires to be enlarged to embrace the population of Upper Canada. With this thought before us, the reply is found in a remembrance that as the rays of the sun and the copious showers of the sky fructify the earth for the equal advantage of every soul, so the State constitution, under which we live and by which we are civilly protected, regards every one as equally entitled to a preservation in his economy of life. There is no *precedence*. Denominational tuition and ecclesiastical discipline are subject respectively to the members composing each organization. And it is a constituent element in law that they be protected in the promulgation of morality and every other quality conducive to happiness and order, always recollecting the often-quoted apothegm that, "Order is heaven's first law; this confessed, some are and must be greater than the rest."

Accordingly, taking up the part enacted by denominations in the separation of Church from State, incomplete as it is, as will be displayed when we come to speak of the Church of England later on, our first inquiry will be the loyalty in kind and degree by which they were affected. The charge preferred was that votes were controlled by the characteristic belief of the denomination, and the intercourse it had with the neighbouring Republic; and that these votes were invariably cast in favour of republican principles.

Taken singly, the Baptists were reputed to be the least reliable in the article of loyalty, and with them we will consort until their case is disposed of and the attitude of another denomination assumed in the controversy is taken up. Statistics and proprietary "holdings" will not be given, for they cannot be had. But knowledge acquired by observation and personal intercourse with families and individuals themselves will be our authority for asserting that the Baptists were not behind other people of Canada in sustaining the British constitution. Side by side with them, numerically compared, I do not know but that they were in advance in what were known as Tory doctrines. This especially so throughout what was known as the Long Point country, Grimsby, and a few other neighbourhoods where this denomination was found.

Of the Baptists it cannot be said they were unpatriotic or selfish, for they promulgated and sustained the declarations—

1st. That State endowments of religion in any form are anti-Scriptural.

2nd. That governments are the result of human necessities, and not the agent or instrument designed of God for the direct or indirect control of religious faith and opinion, which are to be based on the Word of God only.

Every good man is indeed a patriot; for a good man is a public good.

They evidenced their unselfishness, for when they might have obtained from the Government, as a gratuity for their sixty ministers, at least the sum of $38,820, they on principle declined it, and relied solely on the voluntary principle.

Professor J. E. Wells has lately written the life of the Rev. Dr. Fyfe, and in order to give a clear view of the obstacles the Rev. Doctor had to contend against, a review of the Clergy Reserve Question is given, and it, with a quotation from Dent's History of the Rebellion, will constitute our next chapter.

CHAPTER IV.

The Act of 1791—The "Protestant Clergy"—The Imperial Act of 1840—The Episcopal Church Well Cared For—But Not Satisfied—The Question Re-opened—Baptists in the Field.

THE Clergy Reserves had their origin in what is known as the Constitutional Act of 1791. By the thirty-sixth section of that Act provision was made for reserving out of all grants of public lands in Upper and Lower Canada, past as well as future, an allotment for the support of a "Protestant clergy." This allotment was to be "equal in value to the seventh part of the lands so granted." By the next section it was provided that the rents, profits, and emoluments arising from the lands so appropriated were to be applicable solely to the maintenance and support of a Protestant clergy. In these, and companion clauses providing for the endowment of rectories, were enfolded the germs of the worst evils with which the colony was ever afflicted. They were prolific of the bitterest political and sectarian strife. They wrought intolerable hardship and wrong to many industrious settlers. They retarded the growth of the province, hindered the development of its resources, kindled in the bosoms of many of its inhabitants a deep and lasting resentment, and aroused in many others the spirit of hatred, malice, and all uncharitableness. They were the means of arraying those who should have gone forward hand in hand and shoulder to shoulder in the path of material and moral progress, in two hostile camps, and they became eventually one of the exciting causes of the rebellion and bloodshed of 1836.

Such legislation was, of course, wrong in principle, and in any case could have wrought only evil. It involved the noxious element of State-

Churchism, and was, consequently, in itself an infringement on the rights of citizenship, a violation of liberty of conscience, and a gross perversion of the spirit of Christianity. But these inherent evils were intensified by faults of administration and stimulated by the greed of the adherents of the would-be-supreme sect. Those to whom was assigned the duty of making the appropriations, not satisfied with the too liberal provisions of the Act which decreed that the lands reserved for the clergy should be equal to one-seventh of all grants made by the Crown, and so to one-eighth of the whole in which they were included, were accustomed, by a strained interpretation of the clause, to set aside for that purpose one-seventh of the whole, thus making the Clergy Reserves actually equal to one-sixth part of all the lands granted for other purposes. Mr. Dent, in his History of the Rebellion, vol. 1, page 65, adds, that from the fact that this method was confined to about two-thirds of the surveyed townships, as well as from the obvious construction of the statute, "it is to be inferred that the excessive reservations were made deliberately, and not from mere oversight or inadvertence." The surplus thus unjustly appropriated on behalf of the clergy had in 1838 footed up to a total of three hundred thousand acres.

No prophetic powers were needed to foretell the baleful effects of such legislation. The castastrophe was hastened by another vicious practice followed in carrying out the provisions of the Act. Instead of having large blocks set apart in certain localities, the reserves were interspersed amongst the grants made to actual settlers, in order that their value might be enhanced by the improvements made on the contiguous lands. The clergy would thus be doubly endowed, first by the free gift of immense quantities of the public domain, and second, by the large and constant increment resulting from the industry and enterprise of the settlers in the adjacent districts. In some parts, however, as in the Niagara peninsula, and in certain townships along the St. Lawrence, this plan could not be followed, as large grants had already been made *en bloc*. Hence, in these cases, large tracts of neighbouring townships were reserved for the clergy.

The pernicious tendencies of such reservations in either case are apparent. They increase immensely the difficulties of the early settlers in road-making, both for purposes of intercommunication and as a means of reaching the nearest markets. By separating the settlers from each other they become serious barriers to combined action for municipal, school, and other purposes. They debar them, in many cases, from that social intercourse which is so much needed as an alleviation of the hardships of pioneer life. And they do all this in order that the owner of the reserves may be made rich by the improvements wrought by the settlers' toil and privation. The evil effects of such a system of reservations, though some of them are made for more public and juster ends, are seriously felt to-day in Manitoba and the North-West. It would be aside from the object of the present work to dwell upon this aspect of the Clergy Reserves trouble. This brief reference will suffice to show that the people had good reasons, apart altogether from the denominational issues involved, for feeling that the Clergy Reserves were an injustice and an outrage. As a matter of fact, it would seem that the grievance was first felt by the settlers in their private capacity, and that the first protests were uttered and the first combinations formed against the reservations on purely secular grounds.

But murmurs of discontent soon arose in other quarters. The Clergy Reserves became a bone of contention amongst the denominations. The ambiguous wording of the enacting clause made them a veritable apple of discord amongst the various Protestant sects. The dispute turned, of course, on the meaning of the words " Protestant clergy." The word " Protestant," on the one hand, might well be regarded as simply the antithesis of Catholic, and the reserves understood to be for the benefit of all the denominations which abjured the tenets of the Romish Church. But, on the other hand, the word clergy, it was urged, was commonly used in reference to ministers of the established Church of England only, and, it was averred, had never been applied in any British statute to designate any ministers except those of the Churches of Rome and of England. Various other clauses of the Act were adduced in support of the one or the other interpretation. The claim put forward by the Church of Scotland was particularly strong, inasmuch as it was also an established Church in one section of the mother country, and had been expressly recognized as a "Protestant Church" in the Union Act of 1707.

But, it may be asked, can it be that absolutely all the denominations in the Province were engaged in this disgraceful struggle for the loaves and fishes of State endowment? Were there no exceptions to the discreditable rule— no Church, or association of Churches, prepared to take the high New Testament ground and to repudiate all desire or inclination to accept State pay or support? The reply is that, so far as appears, there were no exceptions. The leading denominations at that day were few in number. It was before the "Disruption," and consequently there was no free Presbyterian Church to vindicate, as that Church did nobly a few years later in Canada, the liberty and spirituality of the Church of Christ. The Baptists were as yet few in number and without any organization which could either have demanded its share of the public plunder, or maintained the grand principle of Church independence of which Baptists have been in all ages consistent champions.

The battle raged fiercely. The claims of the Presbyterians were allowed. This was a signal for other Protestant denominations to press their demands for a share of the spoils. The opinions of the constitutional lawyers were invoked to declare the meaning of the Act, and were found to be as various as the views of the bodies which employed them.

Meanwhile, as was to be expected from the

CHURCH AND STATE IN CANADA. 35

fact that the holders of public offices were, almost without exception, members or adherents of that Church, the Episcopalians got the lion's share of the booty. "According to a return to the House of Assembly of lands set apart as glebes in Upper Canada during the forty-six years from 1787 to 1833, it appears that 22,345 acres were so set apart for the clergy of the Church of England, 1,160 acres for ministers of the Kirk of Scotland, 400 for Roman Catholics, and 'none for any other denomination.'"*

It is unnecessary to enter here more minutely into the history of the first Clergy Reserve struggle. After much and fierce contention the question was supposed to be settled by the Imperial Act of 1840, entituled "an Act to provide for the sale of the Clergy Reserves in the Province of Canada, and for the distribution of the proceeds thereof." By this Act the Governor and Council of Canada were empowered to sell the fee simple of the reserves, but not more than

---

* Dent's Rebellion, Vol. I., page 67.

100,000 acres in any one year, and to invest the produce of the same in some public fund, and the interests and dividends on all such investments were to be drawn by the Receiver-General of Canada, and to be paid by him to satisfy all such stipends and allowances as had been made to the clergy of the Churches of England and Scotland, or other religious bodies to which the faith of the Crown was pledged. The amount with which the funds were thus annually chargeable was £9,280. The Act further provided that as soon as the income from the fund should exceed this sum, the interests and dividends accruing from the first of the Clergy Reserve funds, that created by the Act 7 and 8 George IV., should be divided into three equal parts, of which two should be appropriated to the Church of England and one to the Church of Scotland, and those accruing from the second fund, that created by the Act of 1840 above described, should be divided into six equal parts of which two should be appropriated to the Church of England, one to the Church of Scotland, and the remaining three be placed at the disposal of the Governor for the time being, to be applied by him "for purposes of public worship and religious instruction in Canada." Notwithstanding this very favourable settlement of their claims, a settlement which was denounced as unjust by other religious bodies, but acquiesced in for the sake of peace, the English Church authorities were dissatisfied and caused the whole question to be re-opened in 1845, by petitioning the Legislature to have the unsold portions of the reserves divided and the proportion accruing to the Episcopal Church invested in the Church Society of Toronto. This petition, if granted, would, of course, have had the effect of endowing the English Church with immense acres of public lands, and enabling it to withhold them from sale or settlement at pleasure, until such time as the occupation or cultivation of surrounding districts had vastly increased their value. It would, in short, have made the English Church a State-endowed Church, and paved the way for its becoming in fact, what Bishop

Strachan of Toronto actually styled it in a circular letter addressed to the clergy and laity about this date, the "Established Church in Western Canada."

The battle for religious equality, thus indiscreetly renewed by the friends of episcopacy, was waged with vigour and bitterness for several years. It was during this second stage of the conflict that the Baptists entered the arena as an organized body. Mr. Fyfe, though still quite young, took from time to time, as we shall see, an important part in this contest and others of a similar nature. It need scarcely be added that he and other leaders contended not for a share of the spoils, but for absolute civil and religious liberty and equality. They denied the right of other denominations to what they on principle repudiated for themselves, any special privileges purchased for them with the public funds, which were the common property of the whole people, without respect to creed or sect.

Closely connected with the Clergy Reserves trouble was that arising out of the endowed

CHURCH AND STATE IN CANADA. 39

rectories. By sections of the Act of 1791, subsequent to those already referred to, provision was made for the erection and endowment by the Lieutenant-Governor, under instructions from the Crown, of one or more parsonages or rectories in every township, or parish, according to the establishment of the Church of England, and for the presentation of incumbents, subject to the Bishop's right of institution. The stern opposition which the Clergy Reserves provision aroused and the keen contests which ensued year after year, prevented any action being taken to give effect to the clauses respecting the rectories for nearly half a century after the passage of the Act. In view of the fact that the Imperial authorities had requested the Provincial Parliament to legislate on the reserves question with a view to eliminating its more objectionable features, and in view of the further fact that colonial secretaries, and particularly Lord Goderich, had given what were understood to be pledges that no steps would be taken to dispose of any part of the reserves, except in accordance with the views and wishes of a majority of the Canadian people, the public mind seems to have been quite at rest so far as the rectory endowment clauses of the obnoxious Act were concerned. The popular surprise and indignation may be imagined when the fact leaked out that Sir John Colborne, yielding no doubt to the persistent solicitations of his High Church advisers in the Executive Council, had, as one of his last official acts, and only eight days before the arrival of his successor, Sir Francis Head, signed patents creating and endowing forty-four rectories. It afterwards came out that the patents had actually been made out for thirteen more, but had for some reason been left unsigned, and so could not be made available. To the forty-four were assigned more than 17,000 acres of the public lands, an average of nearly 370 acres to each rectory. The transaction was kept secret as long as possible, both from the Home authorities and from the Canadian people. The deed was consummated in January, 1836, but did not become generally known until after the close of the session of Parliament in the spring. For the sequel we cannot do better than quote the concise summary given in a recent historical work :*

"No sooner did it become known than the public indignation began to manifest itself in lurid speeches and newspaper articles. Meetings were held to denounce Sir John Colborne and those who had prompted him to this high-handed iniquity. The Wesleyan Methodist Conference and the Synod of the Church of Scotland in Upper Canada, if agreeing on no other subject, were of one mind as to this, and officially pronounced upon it with a vehemence which commended itself to popular opinion. Petitions without number were sent over the sea. 'The Imperial Government,' says Mr. Lindsey, 'was besieged with petitions, praying for the annulment of the rectories. The temper of the public mind became imbued with that sullenness which a sense of injury begets, and which fore-

---

* Dent's History of the Rebellion, Vol. I., p. 294.

bodes the approach of civil commotion. It was the idea of violated Imperial faith; of a broken compact between the Sovereign and his Canadian subjects, that constituted the sting of the injury. The people recurred to the promise of Lord Goderich that their wishes should be the Sovereign's guide in the matter, and regarded themselves as the victims of a deception which brought dishonour on the Crown and distrust upon Imperial faith.' The Home Government were in two minds about repudiating the transaction. The right of the Lieutenant-Governor to create and endow without the express assent of the King was not perfectly clear, and the law officers of the Crown were consulted on the question. Those gentlemen, on the case submitted for their consideration, pronounced the opinion that there had been an excess of authority; and that the creation and endowment were invalid. Dr. Strachan, upon becoming acquainted with this circumstance, prepared a report embodying certain facts and documents which had not been before the law officers, to whom the case was now submitted a second time. The additional data placed a different face upon the question, and the law officers arrived at a conclusion contrary to that which they had formerly expressed. The grantees were accordingly permitted to retain their property undisturbed, but the name of Sir John Colborne continued to be execrated in Upper Canada for his share in the transaction for many a year."

CHAPTER V.

Methodist Influence—Patriotism—Rev. Wm. Ryerson's Speech—Rev. Dr. Ryerson's Memorandum on the Clergy Reserve Question—Settlement with the Methodists—The Amount of Money the Methodist Clergy Might Have Had But Did Not Take.

IT cannot be denied but that Methodist influences have had a controlling hand in moulding and strengthening the institutions and commerce of our common country.

At an early period in the history of Canada, when they were few in numbers and without the antiquity of organization belonging to those who either ridiculed or maligned their youth and their patriotism, they stood shoulder to shoulder in the ranks which preserved the colony to England. England had her soldiers and navy employed in defending her shores from the aggressions of Napoleonic power, and could ill spare her troops for the purposes of defence along our boundary lines. The militia were our protection; and none came forward with nobler hearts and more valorous determinations than those who wore helmets and cuirasses fashioned with Methodist steel. True patriotism is a species of heroic virtue, and indeed the best species of it, it is said, does not often occur. The name is daily assumed; but by prostitution it as often loses its dignity.

As the last days of the reserves were drawing to a close it fell to the Rev. Wm. Ryerson to repel the equivocal asseverations which had been directed against the people of his own persuasion in respect to the disposal of the reserve funds. They had been styled "enemies of the prosperity of the British Crown." " These hard words," said the speaker, at a public discussion, "were used in reference to 20,000 of the best men of Canada. What were the feelings which these things excited ? Ask that reverend friend (point-. ing to Rev. Mr. Richardson). Rise, sir, (addressing that gentleman), and show that person, once perfect, but shattered and broken and mangled in the service of your country. Tell this audience whether, having fought in a British ship, under a British commander, you have forfeited all claims on the Crown, or whether you are insensible to the value of British institutions. Tell me, ye who say that the opponents of the reserves are enemies to the Crown, how many of those who received medals in honour of their valour and their services in the war with the United States were members of that Church whose petitioners say that they were ignorant or insensible to the fundamental principles of our glorious constitution ?"

These words are nothing more than an inscription upon the flag of the volunteers who adorned and protected Canada, at the moment when, without them, it would have passed to the protectorate of another country. It can be laid down as an axiom that a bad man cannot be a patriot.

On and on went the numerical influence of

these people. Its weight for many years bearing down upon the public mind, is graphically prepared for such a book as this by that State instructor, the Rev. Dr. Ryerson, in a paper of his which he drew up on the 9th of May, 1851, for the guidance of Earl Grey and the Imperial Parliament. It is historic truth, embodied as much in the oratorical language of a Sheridan as in the romance of a poet.

The reverend Doctor was abroad upon educational business at the time of its composition, and, after using the usual formalities of address, he proceeds to say to the Earl:—

Fully concurring in the remark of the Bishop of London, in a late reply to the deputation of the inhabitants of St. George's, Hanover Square, that "there is no kind of intestine division so injurious in its character and tendency as that which is grounded on religious questions"; and firmly believing, as I do, that the long continuance of Canada as a portion of the British Empire depends upon the proceedings of the British Parliament on the question of the Clergy

Reserves, I desire, as a native and resident of Upper Canada, as a Protestant and lover of British institutions, to submit the following brief observations on that question, in order to correct erroneous impressions in England, and to induce such a course of Parliamentary proceedings as will conduce to the honour of Great Britain, and to the peace and welfare of Canada:

1. My first remark is, that this is a question agitated for more than twenty-five years, almost exclusively among Protestants in Canada, and the agitation of which, at the present time, has not, in any way whatever, been promoted by Roman Catholic influence. An attempt has been made in some quarters to create a contrary impression in England; but that I am correct in my statement will, I think, appear from the following facts:—First, though the question of the Clergy Reserves nominally relates to Lower as well as Upper Canada (since the union of the two Canadas under one Legislature), it is historically and practically an Upper Canadian question. The agitation of it originated in

Upper Canada; it never was agitated in Lower Canada before the union of the two provinces; it is discussed chiefly by the Upper Canada press, and pressed most earnestly by the Upper Canada members of the Legislature. So strongly is it viewed as an Upper Canadian question, that a considerable portion of the press of Upper Canada has objected to Lower Canadian members of the Legislature interfering in its discussion or influencing its decision by their votes. Secondly, all the Upper Canadian members, both of the Executive Council and of the Legislative Assembly, are Protestants. Of the forty-two members of the Legislative Assembly elected in Upper Canada, not one of them is a Roman Catholic; of the five Upper Canadian members of the Executive Council, all are Protestants, and all were in favour of the late Address of the Assembly to the Queen, praying for the repeal of the Imperial Act, 4 & 5 Vic., cap. 78, and for restoring to the people of Canada the constitutional right of judging for themselves as to the disposal of the Clergy Reserve lands in that country. It ought, therefore, to be remembered in England, that this question relates chiefly to Upper Canada, which is, for the most part, a Protestant country, and which has not a single Roman Catholic in the Legislative Assembly.

2. I remark, in the next place, that it is not a question of Church and State union, or whether the State shall contribute to the support of religion in one or more forms. It is whether the Canadian people shall judge for themselves as to the mode of supporting their religious worship, as well as to the religious creed they shall adopt. This right was clearly secured to them by their constitutional Act of 1791, 31st George III., cap. 31, but was taken from them by the Imperial Act of 1840, 3 & 4 Vic., cap. 78. In what manner the people of Canada, through their representatives, may exercise the constitutional right, the restoration of which they claim, for the support of religion, I am not prepared to say. But whether they shall exercise wisely or not that, or any other right con-

stitutionally vested in them, is a matter appertaining to themselves, and not to parties in England. I am not to be the less anxious for the restoration to my country of its constitutional rights because it may not exercise them wisely, or exercise them in a manner opposed to my personal views and wishes. The constitutional rights of legislation in Great Britain may not have always been exercised most judiciously, but who would adduce that as an argument for the annihilation of those rights, or against the existence of constitutional freedom in England? Is Canada to be made an exception to this rule?

3. I remark, thirdly, that neither is this a question which affects the vested rights of any parties except those of the people of Canada generally. When one-seventh of the wild lands of Canada was reserved for the support of a Protestant clergy, by the Act of 1791, 31st George III., cap. 31, the Canadian Legislature, created by the same Act, was invested with authority, under certain forms, "to vary or repeal" the several clauses relating to that clergy

land reservation. That vested right the people of Upper Canada possessed from 1791 to 1840. All other vested rights are subordinate to those of a whole people, and are not to be exalted above them. The Canadian Legislative Assembly has proposed to secure all parties who have acquired rights or interests in the revenue arising from the sales of the clergy reserve lands *during the lives of the incumbents or recipients;* but, beyond that guarantee, it claims the right of "varying or repealing," as it shall judge expedient, the landed reservation in question, and the application of the revenues arising from it.

4. The real question for consideration in England being thus separated from other questions with which it has sometimes been erroneously and injuriously confounded, I proceed to remark that the Imperial Act 3 and 4 Vic., cap. 78, is at variance with what the Imperial Governments without exception and without reservation, for twenty-five years, have admitted to be the constitutional rights of the people of Canada. It has at all times been admitted, in the first

place, that the Act 31st Geo. III., cap. 31, which created a Legislature in Canada, and authorized the clergy land reservation, invested the Canadian Legislature with authority to legislate as to its disposal, and the application of revenues arising from it; and, secondly, that whatever legislation might take place on the subject should be in harmony with the wishes of the Canadian people. The Imperial Act 3 and 4 Vic., cap. 78, deprives the Canadian people of that right of legislation which they had possessed for forty years, and does violence to their wishes and opinions in the disposal which it makes of the revenues of the lands in question. Now the rights of the people of Canada on this subject were explicitly stated by the late Sir George Murray in 1828, by the Earl of Ripon in 1832, by His late Most Gracious Majesty in a message to the Legislature of Upper Canada in 1833, and by Lord Glenelg in 1835 and 1836. I give a summary of the whole in the words of Lord Glenelg, in a despatch to the Lieutenant-Governor of Upper Canada, dated December 5,

1835, in reply to an attempt on the part of the latter to induce Imperial legislation on the subject. Lord Glenelg says, on behalf of the Imperial Government, that

Parliamentary legislation on any subject of exclusively internal concern, in a British colony possessing a Representative Assembly, is as a general rule unconstitutional. It is a right of which the exercise is reserved for extreme cases, in which necessity at once creates and justifies the exception.

After showing that no necessity existed for setting aside the constitutional rights of the Canadian people, Lord Glenelg expresses himself in the following language of enlightened political philosophy :—

It is not difficult to perceive the reason which induced Parliament, in 1791, to connect with a reservation of land for ecclesiastical purposes, the special delegation to the Council and Assembly of the right to vary that provision by any Bill which, being reserved for the signification of His Majesty's pleasure, should be communicated to both Houses of Parliament for six weeks before that decision was pronounced. Remembering, it should seem, how fertile a source of controversy ecclesiastical endowment had supplied throughout a large part of the Christian world, and how impossible it was to foretell with precision what might be the prevailing opinions and feelings of the Canadians on this subject at a future period, Parliament at once secured the means of making a systematic provision for a Protestant clergy, and took full precaution against the eventual inaptitude of that system to the more advanced stages of a society then in its infant state, and of which no human foresight could divine the more mature and settled judgment.

In the controversy, therefore, respecting ecclesiastical endowments, which at present divides the Canadian Legislature, I find no unexpected element of agitation, the discovery of which demands a departure from the fixed principles of the constitution, but merely the fulfilment of the anticipations of the Parliament of 1791, in the exhibition of that conflict of opinion for which the statute of that year may be said to have made a deliberate preparation. In referring the subject to the future Canadian Legislature, the authors of the Constitutional Act must be supposed to have contemplated the crisis at which we have now arrived—the era of warm and protracted debate, which, in a free government, may be said to be a necessary precursor to the settlement of any great principle of national policy. We must not have recourse to an extreme remedy, merely to avoid the embarrassment which is the present, though temporary, result of our own legislation.

I think, therefore, that to withdraw from the Canadian to the Imperial Legislature the question respecting the Clergy Reserves, would be an infringement of that cardinal principle of colonial government which forbids Parliamentary interference, except in submission to an evident and well-established necessity.

In January, 1840, the two branches of the Legislature of Upper Canada passed a Bill (the Legislative Assembly by a majority of 28 to 20, and the Legislative Council by a majority of 13 to 4) relative to the Clergy Reserve—providing for the interests of their existing incumbents, and dividing the proceeds of the sales of said lands among various religious persuasions according to a census taken once in five years, and leaving each religious persuasion free to

expend the sum or sums to which it should be
entitled according to its pleasure, whether for
the support of its clergy, the erection of places
of worship, or for purposes of education. Though
the great majority of the people of Upper
Canada desired the application of the proceeds
of these lands for educational purposes only;
yet a majority of both branches of the Legislature agreed to a compromise which could be
defended as just to all parties, whatever preferences might be entertained on the subject in
the abstract. But instead of the Royal assent
being advised to be given to that Canadian Bill
on a local Canadian question, a new Bill was
introduced into the Imperial Parliament, giving
about three-fourths of the proceeds of the Clergy
Reserves (including past and future sales) to the
clergy of the Churches of England and Scotland,
giving nothing to any other Church, but leaving
the remaining one-fourth (or half of future sales)
at the discretionary disposal of the Executive for
religious purposes. This part of the Imperial
Act has proved inoperative to this day; and

should any religious persuasion receive any portion of this comparative pittance of the clergy land funds, it would do so not as a matter of right (as do the Churches of England and Scotland in receiving their lion's share), but at and during the pleasure of any party in power—a position in which no religious community should be placed to the Executive, and in which the Executive ought not to be placed to any religious community. Such an Act can be justified upon no principle of justice or sound policy, and is at variance with the almost unanimous and often recorded wishes of the people of Upper Canada. The *Christian Examiner*—a monthly organ of the Church of Scotland in Upper Canada—expressed not only the general sentiments of the members of that Church, but also of people at large, in the following words, contained in an elaborate editorial which appeared in that publication a few months before the passing of the Imperial Act of 1841 :—

Year after year, at least during the last decade, the general sentiment in this colony has been uttered in no unequivocal form, that no Church invested with exclusive privileges derived from the State, is adapted to the condition of society among us. It cannot be doubted that this is the conviction of nine-tenths of the colonists. Except among a few ambitious magnates of the Church of England, we never hear a contrary sentiment breathed. Equal rights upon equal conditions is the general cry. And although several Assemblymen of the present House have chosen to misinterpret the public voice, and to advocate a different principle, we doubt not that on their next appearance before their constituents, they will be taught that this is not the age, nor this the country, in which the grand principle of equal rights can be departed from with impunity.

Now, although the Imperial Act of 1840 may have induced "a few magnates" of the Church of Scotland to unite with other "magnates," whom they once considered "ambitious," in denying the "grand principle of equal rights" to their more numerous Methodist brethren, and other religious persuasions, yet the "convictions of nine-tenths" of the Canadian people remain unchanged; nor will they, because of the changed circumstances of a few clergymen of the Church of Scotland, suffer "the grand principle of equal rights to be departed from with impunity."

5. I observe, likewise, that the continuance of the Imperial Act of 1840 is desired by a mere fraction of the Canadian population, while its repeal is demanded by that country at large. The assertions of any interested parties on a matter of this kind are of little weight against the proceedings and statements of the representatives of the people. The Address of the Legislative Assembly to Her Majesty must be regarded as the authoritative and true expression of the opinions and wishes of the Canadian people. It is true, there was diversity of opinion as to the manner in which the incumbents on the Clergy Reserve Fund should be dealt with, and also as to certain other declarations contained in the Address of the Assembly; but no member of the Canadian Legislature ventured to justify the provisions of the Imperial Act, and very few ventured to vote in

CHURCH AND STATE IN CANADA. 61

favour of its continuance, even upon the ground of expediency, in behalf of the "magnates" of two favourable Churches. When the resolutions of the Address to Her Majesty were moved in the Legislative Assembly of Canada on this subject, an amendment was moved by the supporters of the present exclusive privileges of the Churches of England and Scotland in Canada, an amendment which contained the following words :—

That in the opinion of this House it is inexpedient to disturb or unsettle, by resolution or enactment, the appropriations or endowments now existing in Upper and Lower Canada for religious purposes; that the well-being of society and the growing wants of the various Christian bodies in Canada demand that the several provisions of the Imperial Act 3 and 4 Vic., cap. 78, should be carried out to their fullest extent.

In favour of the amendment, that is, in favour of the continuance and operations of the Imperial Act of 1840, voted sixteen; against it voted fifty-two. Who would think of perpetuating a law in England at variance with the sentiments of three-fourths of the members of the House of Commons, and even of a large proportion of the constituency of Great Britain? Could the present constitution of Government in England be maintained, could revolution be long prevented, if laws were retained on the statute-book condemned by three-fourths of the Commons, and more than three-fourths of all classes of people in the land, and those statutes involving religious questions? And is that to be perpetuated in Canada which would not be retained in England for a month?

6. Into the origin and progress of the controversy connected with the Clergy Reserves, it is needless for me to enter. They are sufficiently stated in the Address of the Legislative Assembly of Canada to the Queen, a copy of which is herewith annexed, together with the majorities by which each of the thirty-one clauses of the Address was separately voted. It will be seen that the first twenty-three clauses of the Address were carried by a majority of 52 to 18; the 24th clause by 51 to 20; the 26th clause by

48 to 19; the 27th and 28th clauses by 47 to 20; the 29th clause by 36 to 34; the 30th clause by 40 to 28; the 31st clause, containing the prayer of the Address, by 45 to 23. The only clause of the Address, therefore, in favour of which the majority of the Assembly was not large and decided, was the 29th; and in a vote to that clause, I have shown that the smallness of the majority was occasioned by objections to different parts of the clause upon quite opposite grounds, of three classes of members—the sixteen supporters of the present pre-eminence of the Churches of England and Scotland, a section of the Roman Catholic members, and what in England would be called the extreme dissenters. In the vote referred to, I have explained the ground of the opposition to this clause by each of these three classes of members. It will be seen that the 29th clause is rather speculative than practical, and does not affect the character and completeness of the Address, every other clause of which was carried by a large majority. It is, however, curious to remark, that while the

supporters of the present exclusive privileges of the Churches of England and Scotland are indebted to the assistance of Roman Catholic members for the only vote in which the minority was large; yet in England some of these same parties represent the Address as having been carried chiefly by Roman Catholic votes, with a view of destroying all Protestant institutions in Canada.

7. No enlightened and candid person can look at the religious history and social state of Canada and desire the perpetuation of the Imperial Act 3 and 4 Vic., cap. 78. It is now quite sixty years since Upper Canada was formed into a province with a representative government. Its population was then 7,000 souls; it is now about 700,000. During the first and most eventful half of that sixty years, the ministrations of the Churches of England and Scotland can scarcely be said to have had an existence there. The present Bishop of Toronto, in a discourse published on the occasion of the death of the first Canadian Bishop of the Church of

England, states that down to the close of the war between Great Britain and the United States in 1815, there were but four resident clergymen or missionaries of the Church of England in all Upper Canada—a statement which is confirmed by the annual reports of the Society for the Propagation of the Gospel in Foreign Parts; and the same reports will show how few were the clergy of the Church of England in that province down to a recent period. We learn from the same authority, that till 1818 there was but one clergyman of the Church of Scotland in Upper Canada, and that in 1827 there were but two. It is, therefore, clear that during the first half of its sixty years' existence as a province, Upper Canada must have been indebted almost entirely to other than clergy of the Churches of England and Scotland for religious instruction; yet during that thirty years, it is admitted that the people of Upper Canada were a religious, an intelligent, and loyal people. To whom the people of that province were mainly indebted for their religious instruction, and for the formation and development of their religious character, appears in a report of a Select Committee of the Upper Canada House of Assembly, appointed in 1828, on the religious condition of the country, and before which fifty witnesses, chiefly members of the Church of England, were examined. I quote the following words from the report of that Committee (which was adopted by the Assembly by a majority of 22 to 8), a report which was partly prepared in reference to a letter addressed by the present Bishop of Toronto to His Majesty's Secretary of State for the Colonies in 1827 :—

The insinuations (says the report) in the letter against the Methodist clergymen, the committee have noticed with peculiar regret. To the disinterested and indefatigable exertions of these pious men this Province owes much. At an early period of its history, when it was thinly settled, and destitute of all other means of religious instruction, these ministers of the Gospel, animated by Christian zeal and benevolence, at the sacrifice of health and interest and comfort, carried among the people the blessings and consolations and sanctions of our holy religion. Their influence and instruction have been conducive, in a degree which cannot be easily estimated, to the reformation of the vicious and to the diffusion of correct morals, the foundation of all sound loyalty and social order.

This religious body has now 180 regular ministers in Upper Canada, about 1,100 churches and preaching places, and embraces in its congregations one-seventh of the population.* Yet this oldest religious community in Upper Canada, together with the Free Presbyterian Church of Canada, the United Presbyterian Church, the Baptists and Congregationalists, are treated as nobody by the Imperial Act, while the more modern Churches of England and Scotland are exclusively endowed, and that by setting aside legislative rights which the Constitution of 1791 had conferred upon the people of Upper Canada! In Great Britain the Established Churches are associated with the early and brightest period of

---

* Since the foregoing was written, it has been ascertained that the Wesleyan Methodists number 142,000, or more than one-fifth of the entire population (1850).

British history, and are blended with all the influences which distinguish and exalt British character; but the feelings and predilections arising from such reminiscences and associations are not the proper rule of judgment as to the feelings, predilections and institutions of Canadian society. As Englishmen best know their own feelings and wants, and claim and exercise the sole right of judging and legislating for themselves, so do the people of Canada best know their own wishes and interests, and ought to judge and legislate for themselves in all local matters which do not infringe any Imperial prerogative. No Englishman can refuse this who wishes to do to others as he would have others do to him.

8. But it should also be observed, that down to the passing of the Imperial Act of 1840, the influence of the Church of Scotland itself was adverse to any such act of partiality and injustice, and in favour of applying the proceeds of the Clergy Reserves even to educational as well as religious purposes. The discussion of

this question was first introduced into the Legislative Assembly of Upper Canada in 1823, by the Hon. William Morris—a gentleman of great respectability, and who has always been regarded and acknowledged as the guardian of the interests, and representative of the sentiments, of the Church of Scotland. December 22nd, 1826, Mr. Morris moved a series of resolutions on this subject, of which the following are the 9th and 10th :—

9. *Resolved,*—That it is the opinion of a great proportion of the people of this Province that the clergy lands, in place of being enjoyed by the clergy of an inconsiderable part of the population, ought to be disposed of, and the proceeds of their sale applied to increase the provincial allowance for the support of district and common schools, and the endowment of a provincial seminary for learning, and in aid of erecting places of public worship for all denominations of Christians. [Carried by a majority of 31 to 2.]

10. *Resolved,*—That it is expedient to pass a Bill, authorizing the sale of the clergy lands within this Province, for the purposes set forth

in the foregoing resolution; and to address His Majesty, humbly soliciting that he will be graciously pleased to give the Royal assent to said Bill. [Carried by a majority of 30 to 3.]

On the 28th of the same month, Mr. Morris reported a draft of Bill for the sale of the Clergy Reserves, pursuant to the foregoing resolutions. The Bill passed the Assembly by a majority of 20 to 3; was sent to the Legislative Council, and was rejected. Similar attempts to legislate having in like manner and from the same cause proved abortive, another address to the King on this subject was adopted by the Assembly in March, 1831, and supported, if not introduced, by Mr. Morris. That address, which was adopted by a majority of 30 to 7, contains the following words:—

That a large majority of the inhabitants of this Province are sincerely attached to your Majesty's person and Government, but are averse to any exclusive or dominant Church. That this House feels confident that, to promote the prosperity of this portion of your Majesty's dominions, and to satisfy the earnest desire of the people of this Province, your Majesty will be graciously pleased to give the most favourable consideration to the wishes of your faithful subjects. That, to terminate the jealousy and dissension which have hitherto existed on the subject of the said Clergy Reserves—to remove a barrier to the settlement of the country, and to provide a fund available for the promotion of education, and in aid of erecting places of worship for various denominations of Christians: it is extremely desirable that the said land reserve should be sold, and the proceeds arising from the sale of the same placed at the disposal of the Provincial Legislature, to be applied exclusively for those purposes.

This address was replied to the January following, 1832, by a formal message from the King, from which I extract the following sentences :—

The representations which have at different times been made to His Majesty and his Royal predecessors of the prejudice sustained by his faithful subjects in Upper Canada, from the appropriation of the Clergy Reserves, have engaged His Majesty's most attentive consideration. . . It has, therefore, been with peculiar satisfaction that, in his inquiries into this subject, His Majesty has found that the changes sought for by so large a portion of the inhabitants of Upper Canada, may be carried into effect without sacrificing the just claims of the established Churches of England and Scotland. . . . His Majesty, therefore, invites the House of Assembly of Upper Canada to consider how the powers given the Provincial Legislature by the Constitutional Act to vary or repeal this part of its provisions, can be called into exercise most advantageously, for the spiritual and temporal interests of His Majesty's faithful subjects in the Province.

It will be seen that the Address to the Crown and reply, above quoted, contemplated the application of no part of the proceeds of the clergy lands for the support of the clergy of any religious persuasion, but the application of the whole to the promotion of education, and in aid of erecting places of worship. I do not make these references to advocate this view of the question, but to show that the Crown has long since assented to the alienation of the whole of the proceeds of the reserves from the support of the clergy of any Church, should the Canadian Legislature think proper to do so, and that the Church of Scotland in Upper Canada agreed with the other religious persuasions, and the great majority of the Canadian people, in the advocacy of such an alienation of said reserves. The same parties cannot now object on constitutional and moral grounds to what they heretofore advocated on those same grounds.

9. It has, however, been alleged that the people of Canada have acquiesced in the provisions of the Imperial Act, and are satisfied with it. At the time of passing the Imperial Act, in 1840, and down to within the last two years, the discussion of questions relating to the organization and system of government itself occupied the attention of the public mind in Canada; but no sooner was the public mind set at rest on those paramount and fundamental questions, than the Canadian people demanded the restoration of their rights on the question of the Clergy Reserves. What they have felt for two years, and often and strongly spoken,

through the local press and at the hustings, they now speak in the ears of the Sovereign of the Imperial Parliament. That there must be deep and general dissatisfaction in Canada on this subject, will appear from the following circumstances: (1) The Imperial Act infringes the rights, and contravenes the wishes of the Canadian people; (2) It inflicts an injustice and wrong upon the great majority of the religious persuasions in that country, where the "convictions of nine-tenths" or rather ninety-nine one-hundredths, of the inhabitants are in favour of "equal rights upon equal conditions," among all classes and persuasions; (3) The Legislative Assembly, by a majority of 51 to 20, declare that the Imperial Act, "so far from settling this long agitated question, has left it to be the subject of renewed and increased public discontent;" (4) The comparative silence of the Wesleyan body—the oldest, the most numerous, and the most unjustly treated, of all the excluded denominations—is expressive and ominous. Its representatives, having proceeded to England in

1840, remonstrated against this Bill, then before Parliament; they sought the assent of Her Majesty's Secretary of State for the Colonies to be heard at the Bar of the House of Commons against it, and having been refused, they presented to him, July 27th, 1840, a most earnest remonstrance against the Bill. On the Bill becoming law, they silently submitted, and on grounds which were explained, a few months since, by the official organ of the Wesleyan Methodist Church in Canada, in the following words:—

On Lord John Russell's Bill becoming law, the question was changed from a denominational to a Provincial one—from an ecclesiastical to a constitutional one. It was no longer a question between one denomination and another, but a question between Upper Canada and the Imperial Parliament. As Canadians, and acting in behalf of a large section of the Canadian community, the representatives of the Wesleyan Methodist Church expressed their convictions, their feelings, and their apprehensions to Her Majesty's Government while the question was pending before Parliament; but when the excerable Bill became an Imperial law, it was as much out of place for them as clergymen, or of any religious persuasion, to strive to fulfil their own predictions, or set on foot a Colonial civil contest, as it would have been pusillanimous in them not to have remonstrated before the consummation of such an act of wrong against the people of Upper Canada. The question is now being taken up in the right place, and, we trust, in the right spirit.

10. Under such circumstances it is impossible that the question can long remain in its present state, and it is for the Imperial Parliament to say what shall be done. It is admitted upon all hands that the members of the Churches of England and Scotland in Canada are more wealthy in proportion to their numbers, and, therefore, less needful of extraneous aid than the members of any other religious persuasion; and in proportion to their numbers and wealth will be their comparative influence and advantages in the proceedings of their own Legislature. It is a grave question, whether the Imperial Parliament will place itself in an attitude

of hostility to the Legislative Assembly and people of Canada for the sake of conferring questionable pecuniary distinctions upon the clergy of the two most wealthy denominations in that country? Should any members of Parliament be disposed to pursue this course, and hazard this experiment, I beg them to pause and consider the following questions :—

(1) Can the real interests of the Churches of England and Scotland themselves be advanced by occupying a position of antagonism to the acknowledged equal rights of the great majority of the people of Canada? And is it desirable that these Churches should be the instruments and emblems of wrong to a country, rather than natural and powerful agencies of its unity, advancement, and happiness? Interested parties in Canada may not be able to see this, but British and Canadian statesmen ought not to overlook it.

(2) Ought the members of the Churches of England and Scotland, who take a part in public affairs in Canada, and who may be candidates

for popular power, to be placed in circumstances in which they must either war against the position and authorities of their own Church, or war against all other religious persuasions, or retire from public life altogether?

(3) What will be the natural, or apparently inevitable, result of thus singling out two classes of Canadian people, and distinguishing them from all others by pecuniary endowments, and sustaining them in that position, not by the free Legislature of their own country—not by the original principles of their constitution of government to which Canada may have pledged itself —but by a recent Imperial Act, to the preparing or provisions of which the Canadians were no parties, and against which they protest? Is it likely that the will or predilections of a transatlantic House of Lords, so largely composed of and influenced by one class of ecclesiastical dignitaries, can long determine the mutual relations of religious persuasions in a country constituted as Canada is, and bordering on the northern free Anglo-States of America? What

the Canadians ask they ask on grounds originally guaranteed to them by their constitution ; and if they are compelled to make a choice between British connection and British constitutional rights, it is natural that they should prefer the latter to the former ? It is also to be noted that the Imperial Act in question has to be administered through the local Canadian administration. Such is the machinery of the Act. The revenue that it appropriates is Canadian, and it is worked through Canadian agency—through Canadian heads of departments, responsible to the representatives of the people of Canada. Should the Canadian people, then, find that their respectful and earnest appeal to the Imperial Parliament, through the Sovereign, is in vain, they will naturally look to their own resources and elect representatives at the ensuing general elections who will pledge themselves to oppose the administration of the Imperial Act—representatives who will support no Inspector or Receiver-General that will be responsible for the payment of even any warrant for moneys under such Act. The consequence must soon be, not only injury to existing incumbents whom the Canadian Assembly now propose to secure, but collision between the Government and the Legislative Assembly, and ultimately between the latter and the Imperial authorities; and finally, either the establishment of military government in Canada (an impossibility), or the severance of that great country from Great Britain. On the other hand, if the reasonable demand and constitutional rights of the people of Canada be regarded in this question, I believe Canada will remain freely and cordially connected with the Mother Country for many years, if not generations, to come. I will conclude these observations in the expressive words of Lord Stanley, to the spirit of which I hope every British statesman will respond. On the 2nd of May, 1828, in a speech on this subject, Lord Stanley expressed himself in the following terms :—

That if any exclusive privileges be given to the Church of England, not only will the measure be repugnant to every principle of sound legislation, but contrary to the spirit and intention of the Act of 1791, under which the reserves were made for the Protestant clergy. I will not enter further into it at present, except to express my hope that the House will guard Canada against the evils which religious dissensions have already produced in this country and in Ireland, where we have examples to teach us what to shun. We have seen the evil consequences of this system at home. God forbid we should not profit by experience; and more especially in legislating for a people bordering on a country where religious intolerance and religious exclusions are unknown—a country to which Parliament looked in passing the Act of 1791, as all the great men who argued the question then expressly declared. It is important that His Majesty's Canadian subjects should not have occasion to look across the narrow boundary that separates them from the United States, to see anything there to envy.

It cannot be shown that the Methodists received any advantage from the settlement of the Reserve question, as did the Church of England and the Presbyterians, because their main contention was in favour of education, and they omitted to put in a claim, as they might have done, for 215 of their ordained ministers. Certainly from time to time they obtained grants from the Government in aid of their mission work and educational enterprises; and at the cessation of legislative enactments they got $39,074.17 appropriated in sustentation of Indian missions. But that their ministers did forego, on strictly voluntary principles, a claim for $1,395,483, if the Presbyterian and Church of England basis be taken as one upon which to calculate, is very apparent. Indeed, this is a fact for which they have not heretofore received any credit.

CHAPTER VI.

Clergy Reserve Controversies in Canada, 1817-1831—
Original Grant of Lands in 1791 for the Support of a
Protestant Clergy—Proposal to Alienate Them made
in 1817—Episcopal Clergy Corporations Established
—Exclusive Claims of Church of England—Petition
of Dr. Strachan, as Chairman of Clergy Corporation,
in 1823, and appended Ecclesiastical Chart—Action
of Legislative Assembly in 1825-1826—Grant of £750
to Scottish Clergy—King's College Charter : Its Sectarian Character—Dr. Strachan's Letter and Ecclesiastical Chart of 1827—Investigation by Committee of
Imperial House of Commons—Letters of Bishop of
Quebec and of Scottish Clergy on the Clergy Reserves
in 1827-1828—Claims of Clergy of the United Presbytery of Upper Canada—Ultimate Disposal of the
Clergy Reserves.

ASSOCIATED with this chapter is the wish we had to include a short biographical sketch of such men as, by a life of self-denying piety and excellent principles, distinguished themselves in the country of their birth or adoption. With regret we are compelled to omit them, for to name a part would not be fair to the whole. Their history would make a volume equally pleasant to read and conducive to a desire for the information which warms the spirit of a Christian and stimulates the activity and intelligence of a citizen.

The Rev. Dr. Gregg, Professor of Apologetics and Church History in Knox College, Toronto, has written a book upon the "History of the Presbyterian Church in Canada," and from it the following pages are taken :—

The chief parties in the controversy were the clergy and adherents of the Church of England, who claimed an exclusive right to the Clergy Reserves; the clergy and people of the Church of Scotland, who claimed equal rights with the Church of England; and the clergy and people of the United Presbytery and Synod, who also considered themselves entitled to share in the provision made for a Protestant clergy. The Methodist and other Churches also took part in the conflict. Among politicians the battle was keenly waged; the Tories siding with the Church of England in its exclusive claims, while the Reformers favoured a more liberal policy. Opposite sides also were taken by the Legislative Council, which was appointed by the Crown, and the Legislative Assembly, which was elected by the people; the Council adopting the exclusive and the Assembly the liberal views. Before the era of responsible government the influence of the Lieutenant-Governors was generally, and sometimes very decidedly, exercised in favour of the exclusive claims of the Church of England.

By the Treaty of Paris, in 1763, the Roman Catholic Church in Canada was allowed to retain its extensive ecclesiastical property, and, by an Imperial Act in 1774, it was confirmed in its possession. But the interests of Protestants were not neglected. By the Act of 1774 it was provided that it should be lawful for His Majesty, his heirs and successors, to make provision " for the encouragement of the Protestant religion, and for the maintenance and support of a Protestant clergy." In the year 1791, the thirty-first of the reign of George III., an Act was passed by the British Parliament, usually called the Constitutional Act, by which Upper and Lower Canada were erected into separate Provinces. By the thirty-sixth clause of this Act the seventh part of the unceded lands in both Provinces was reserved "for the support and maintenance of a Protestant clergy." As the Crown lands were ceded the reserves were to be made. Within a few years after the passing of the Act upwards of three millions of acres were allocated as Clergy Reserves; the number of acres in Upper Canada was 2,395,687, and in Lower Canada 934,052.

For many years after these lands were set apart they yielded little or no revenue, and scarcely any notice was taken of them. But in the course of time they became more valuable, and in 1817 public attention was specially called to them in the Legislative Assembly by Mr. Robert Nichol in a series of resolutions, one of which proposed that the Imperial Parliament should be petitioned to sell a part of the lands already reserved, and that a less proportion than one-seventh should be reserved for the future. The discussion of these proposals was prevented by Governor Gore suddenly and prematurely proroguing Parliament. About this time Dr. Mountain, Bishop of Quebec, seems to have taken an active part in the disposal of the Clergy Reserves, as appears from a letter of Earl Bathurst, Secretary of State for the Colonies, dated 2nd April, 1818, to Mr. President Smith. Lord Bathurst says that the Bishop had frequently brought under his consideration the advantages which would result to the Church of England in the Province of Upper Canada from the legal establishment of parishes and rectories; that he concurred in this view, and that he had received the commands of the Prince Regent to instruct Mr. Smith to take the necessary legal measures for constituting and erecting rectories and parishes in every township within the Province. The endowment of the rectories was to be made a matter for future consideration; and, until the more general settlement of the Province, the management of the reserves should be vested in a corporate body, or continue under the control of the Lieutenant-Governor and Executive Council. In the following year Bishop Mountain applied to the Imperial Government to have the direction of the Clergy Reserves placed in the hands of the Episcopal clergy. The application was successful; clergy corporations were created in each of the Provinces, with power to lease and receive rents for the lands, but not to sell them. The corporations consisted of the Bishop and his clergy, who, by their appointment, derived the advantage of seeming to be the owners of what they were appointed to superintend. Previous to their appointment the annual income from the reserves was £700; under their management it was reduced in a few years to £150.

Hitherto nothing seems to have been done by the Presbyterians to secure their interests in the Clergy Reserves. But on the 17th May,

1819, the Presbyterian inhabitants of the town of Niagara presented a petition to Sir Peregrine Maitland, Lieutenant-Governor of Upper Canada, representing that their church had been burned by the American army during the late war; that they had again erected a temporary place of worship; that they were now destitute of a stated minister, and were anxious to obtain one from the Established Church of Scotland if possible, and that having suffered many losses they were unable to pay an adequate stipend; they therefore prayed that His Excellency would take their peculiar case into consideration, and grant them the annual sum of £100 in aid, "out of the funds arising from Clergy Reserves, or any other fund" at His Excellency's disposal. In transmitting this petition to Earl Bathurst, the Lieutenant-Governor informs him that the actual product of the Clergy Reserves is about £700 per annum, and adds: "This petition involves a question on which, I perceive, there is a difference of opinion, namely, whether the Act intends to extend the benefit of the reserves for the maintenance of a Protestant clergy to all denominations, or only to those of the Church of England." The question was submitted by Earl Bathurst without delay to His Majesty's law officers in England for their opinion, which was given on the 15th November, 1819, and which contains the following clause: "We are of opinion that though the provisions made by 31 Geo. III., chap. 31, ss. 36 and 42, for the support and maintenance of a Protestant clergy, are not confined solely to the clergy of the Church of England, but may be extended also to the clergy of the Church of Scotland, if there be any such settled in Canada (as appears to have been admitted in the debate upon the passing of the Act), yet they do not extend to the Dissenting ministers, since, we think, the term 'Protestant clergy' can apply only to Protestant clergy recognized and established by law." It was thus clearly the opinion of the law officers of the Crown that the clergy of the Church of Scotland were entitled to a share in the Clergy Reserves. It may here be mentioned, with reference to the

Act of 1791, which was introduced by Mr. Pitt, that the Earl of Harrowby stated in the House of Lords in 1828 that he had had repeated conversations with Lord Grenville, who had requested him, if any opportunity should offer, to state "that both his own and Mr. Pitt's decision was that the provisions of 31 Geo. III. were not intended for the exclusive support of the Church of England, but for the maintenance of the clergy generally of the Protestant Church." Viscount Sandon also testified, in 1828, before a committee of the House of Commons, that he understood Lord Grenville to say "that the distinction of a Protestant clergy, which is frequently repeated in the Act of 1791, was meant to provide for any clergy that was not Roman Catholic." This testimony he gave in order to rectify a reported conversation with him, given by Dr. Strachan, rector of York, in a speech delivered in the Legislative Council in Canada in 1828.

On the 6th May, 1820, Earl Bathurst wrote to Sir P. Maitland informing him that His Majesty's law officers were of opinion that though the provisions of the Act of 1791 were not confined solely to the clergy of the Church of England, but might be extended also to the clergy of the Church of Scotland, yet that they did not extend to all Dissenting ministers. The knowledge of this opinion, and of its transmission to the Colonial Governor, seems to have been withheld or concealed from the public for years. The Hon. William Morris, who took a deep interest and active part in the Clergy Reserves controversy, referring to what took place in 1826, says: "Little did I dream, at the period alluded to, that an opinion in support of the rights of the Church of Scotland had previously been furnished to Earl Bathurst by His Majesty's legal advisers;" and so late as 1838 Mr. Morris was unaware that this opinion had been transmitted to the Government of the colony. At all events the opinion of the law officers of the Crown was practically disregarded by Sir P. Maitland and his advisers, as will afterwards appear.

CHURCH AND STATE IN CANADA. 93

On the 22nd of February, 1823, the Earl of Dalhousie, Governor-General of Canada, transmitted to Earl Bathurst copies of two letters which he had received from the ministers of the Scotch churches at Quebec and Lochiel with a view to an additional provision for the support of the clergy of these churches. In his reply Lord Bathurst admits the justice and propriety of many of the remarks of the minister of Lochiel, but says that he is not aware of any funds from which the asked-for provision could be made; and that he does not think it would be expedient or just to apply to the Assembly for a provision for the Scotch clergy, unless at the same time a proposition was made for the support of the English Protestant clergy within the Province, who were placed in the most anomalous situation, and part of whose income was derived from the military chest, and the charge included in the army extraordinaries. He also expresses his fear " that there would be little disposition in the House of Commons to sanction any increase of that necessary charge which must be sustained at home for the support of the English Protestant Church in Lower Canada, for whom no effective provision is made within the Colony, however desirable it might be to afford the ministers of the Scotch Church that assistance which their exemplary conduct so much deserves." At this time the Episcopal clergy in Lower Canada were receiving from public funds upwards of £5,000 yearly, while the whole amount given to the Presbyterian clergy of both Provinces was £50 each to two ministers in Quebec and Montreal, who acted as military chaplains, and £100 each to Mr. Bell, of Perth, and Mr. Henderson, of St. Andrews.

On the 25th April, 1823, Governor Maitland transmitted to Earl Bathurst copies of petitions addressed to the King, Lords and Commons by Dr. Strachan, as chairman of the Upper Canada Clergy Reserves Corporation, and dated York, 22nd April, 1823. The petition to the House of Lords is in many respects an extraordinary document. It represents that the petitioners had recently heard of a petition to the Imperial

Parliament from the ministers of the Church of
Scotland in the Canadas, praying for a share in
the benefits arising from the lands reserved for
the support of a Protestant clergy; that they
are therefore seriously alarmed, not only for the
rights of the Church of England, but for the
cause of religion itself; that they are unaware
of the arguments by which such an extraordinary
claim is attempted to be established, but feel
convinced that a plain statement of facts will
invalidate the allegations of their opponents
and preserve the rights of the Church of England. What are represented as facts are such
as the following:—That the Province of Upper
Canada was settled by Loyalists from the United
States, who were chiefly Episcopalians "ever
distinguished in the Colonies on account of their
affection for the parent State and their incor-
ruptible attachment to the King;" that the
population still retains its prominent feature of
being attached to the Church of England; that
comparatively little progress has been made by
other denominations; that the number of clergy-

men of the "Established Church" in Upper Canada is twenty-two; that a list of more than thirty students now lies before the petitioners, and that many more young men than can possibly be provided for are presenting themselves to the Lord Bishop as candidates for holy orders; that the Lutheran clergymen have generally conformed to the Church of England, and brought their congregations with them; that "several Presbyterian or Congregational clergymen, for both names are used promiscuously in this country, have solicited the Lord Bishop to be admitted as candidates for holy orders;" "that with the exception of the Methodists, who have been deserted by their brethren in England, and left for instruction to itinerants from the United States, there appears no prominent denomination of Protestants but the Established Church capable of exciting public attention, for the Congregationalists or Independent Presbyterians, who are next in number to the Methodists, have only six small congregations, the teachers of whom have lately assumed the appellation of the 'Presbytery of the Canadas' for the purpose of giving themselves importance, and consist of two Irish Presbyterians, one Scotch Seceder, one English Independent and two American Congregationalists;" that the members of the Kirk of Scotland are the fewest in number of any Protestant denomination in Upper Canada, and possessed only one congregation in the Province from 1784 to 1822; that they attempted, without success, to form a second congregation in Kingston in 1822, and that there is no appearance in any other part of the Province of a third in communion with the Kirk of Scotland. With respect to the claim of the ministers of the Church of Scotland to a share in the Clergy Reserves, the petitioners contend that the words "Protestant clergy" in the Act of 1791 are used as contra-distinguishing the clergy of the Church of England from the clergy of the Church of Rome, and cannot be further extended without producing the greatest confusion, for say they: "After passing the Church of England where shall their meaning terminate? Congregationalists, Seceders, Irish Presbyterians, Baptists, Methodists, Moravians, Universalists, will undoubtedly prefer their claims, as they are each more numerous than the Presbyterians in communion with the Kirk of Scotland." They further urge that the construction always put on the Act by themselves and the members of the Church of England is unequivocally confirmed by His Majesty's instructions, which declare in express words that the powers and privileges of an Established Church in the Canadas belong only to the Protestant Church of England, which declaration necessarily excludes the Church of Scotland from all participation in the reserved lands. They deprecate the evils of disunion, competition and disloyalty which must result from setting up a new and rival religious establishment in Canada, and humbly pray, and fervently hope, that the House of Lords will not entertain a petition so manifestly injurious to the rights and interests of the Church of England, and so fraught, in their judgment, with ill consequences to the inhabitants of the Province as that which they have been informed has been brought before their lordships by ministers of the Church of Scotland residing in Canada.

To the petition of the Clergy Corporation is appended an Ecclesiastical Chart, in which are given the names of twenty clergymen of what is called the "Established Church"; of six of what is called the "Independent Presbyterian order, assuming the appellation of the Presbytery of the Canadas," and of four in connection with the Kirk of Scotland. The Rev. Messrs. Johnston, Smart, Bell, McDowall, Harris and Jenkins are the clergymen said to belong to the Independent Presbyterian order, and the Rev. Messrs. McKenzie, McLaurin, Leith and Barclay the clergymen in connection with the Church of Scotland. "As the Methodists (it is added) have no settled clergymen it has been found difficult to ascertain the number of itinerants employed, but it is presumed to be considerable, perhaps ten or twelve in the whole Province. The other denominations appear to have very few teachers, and these seemingly very ignorant."

It will be noticed that the exclusive claims set forth in the petition are directly in conflict with the opinion of the law officers of the Crown communicated to Governor Maitland, with which it can scarcely be conceived that Dr. Strachan, his chief adviser, was unacquainted. It will be noticed also that in the petition one of the Presbyterian ministers (Mr. Smart) is described as an English Independent, and two others (Messrs. McDowall and Jenkins) as American Congregationalists, and that no mention is made of several Presbyterian ministers then settled in Upper Canada, such as Messrs. Eastman, Boyd, Buchanan and Gemmell. It will be noticed also that the number of itinerant Methodist ministers is estimated at about ten or twelve, while, in point of fact, there were more than twenty-four in the Province. It will still further be noticed that insinuations are thrown out against the loyalty of others than Episcopalians, and that it is intimated that if the clergy of the Church of Scotland are permitted to share the benefits of the Clergy Reserves disunion and disaffection will be the necessary results. It is easy to understand how the adoption of such methods as those employed in this petition, and afterwards resorted to, when made known to the public, tended to mar the progress and impair the moral influence of the Church whose interests they were intended to serve, and at the same time to produce the disaffection which the Clergy Corporation seemed so anxious to prevent.

On the 16th of December, 1823, a series of resolutions was introduced into the Legislative Assembly of Upper Canada by the Hon. William Morris. These were designed to counteract the exclusive policy of the Clergy Corporation and protect the interests of the Church of Scotland, whose claim to an equality of rights in the benefits of the Clergy Reserves was founded on the Articles of Union between England and Scotland. The resolutions were adopted by the Assembly. The following is a copy of them :—

Resolved,—That when the kingdoms of England and Scotland were united the subjects of both were placed upon a footing of reciprocity, and were to enjoy a full communication of every right, privilege and advantage, and that neither the Church of the one nor of the other thereby gained an ascendency—on the contrary, that both were established by law as national Protestant Churches within their respective kingdoms, and consequently the clergy of both are equally entitled to a participation in all the advantages which have resulted, or may hereafter result, from the said union.

Resolved,—That the Provinces of Canada were wrested from the dominion of France by the united exertions of Great Britain and Ireland, and that the Churches of England and Scotland had at the conquest thereof an equal claim to enjoy the advantages which might be derived from the said conquest.

Resolved,—That by the Act of the British Parliament passed in the thirty-first year of his late Majesty's reign, the Governor, Lieutenant-Governor, or person administering the government of this Province, was authorised to set apart a portion of one-seventh of the land for the support and maintenance of a Protestant clergy.

CHURCH AND STATE IN CANADA. 103

Resolved,—That if His Majesty, when he graciously authorised an appropriation of land to the support and maintenance of a Protestant clergy in this Province, did not contemplate a provision for the clergy of the Church of Scotland, that they ought now to come under His Majesty's most favourable consideration by being otherwise provided for.

Resolved,—That an humble address be presented to His Majesty, formed on the foregoing resolutions, praying that His Majesty will be graciously pleased to direct such measures as will secure to the clergy of the Church of Scotland residing, or who may hereafter reside, in this Province such support and countenance as His Majesty shall think proper.

An address was accordingly prepared, and in due time transmitted for presentation to His Majesty. It was not concurred in by the Legislative Council, five members of that body voting for it and six against it. Mr. Morris attributes its failure to receive the support of the Council to the fact that the opinion of the law officers of the Crown was still unknown by the public. "I am firmly persuaded (he says) that it would have received the assent of both branches had the fact been known to the public that the law officers of the Crown had recently given an opinion in accordance with the view taken of the law by the Assembly." Before transmitting the address of the Assembly, Governor Maitland wrote a long despatch to Earl Bathurst, dated 27th December, 1823, in which he echoes the opinions of the Clergy Corporation, strenuously endeavouring to establish the exclusive claims of the Church of England to the Clergy Reserves, and setting forth the evil results to be apprehended from conceding the claims of the Church of Scotland. It would seem from this despatch that Governor Maitland had completely forgotten, or had not the slightest regard for, the opinion of the law officers of the Crown, in favour of the Church of Scotland, which Earl Bathurst had transmitted in 1820.

The address of the Legislative Assembly was transmitted by Governor Maitland on the 21st January, 1824, in a brief despatch, in which he referred to his despatch of the 27th December, as conveying his sentiments on the subject of the Clergy Reserves. Within two weeks he took a new method, in conjunction with Dr. Strachan, to forward the aims of the Clergy Corporation. On the 4th of February he wrote to Lord Bathurst informing him that Dr. Strachan intended to visit England "solely on his private affairs," but that he had requested him to be the bearer of a proposition, which Dr. Strachan had himself reduced to writing, at his (the Governor's) suggestion, and commending the Doctor "as a person well able to furnish complete and authentic information respecting the Clergy Reserves." The document containing the proposals commences with historical references to the American Revolution, the special loyalty of Episcopalians and the Constitutional Act of 1791. It proceeds to explain the reasons why but a small proportion of the Clergy Reserve lands had been leased, and why it was hoped that a much larger proportion would be leased in future years. It states that at the present time £30,000 per annum would be needed to sustain an adequate supply of clergymen of the Church of England in Upper Canada, that £60,000 would be needed in twenty-one years, and that this amount could not be obtained from the rents of leased lands. It was therefore proposed, in order to secure the necessary funds, to empower the Clergy Corporation to sell as well as lease the Clergy Reserve lands, and to place the money arising from the sales in the British funds, the interest to be applied to the support of the clergy of the Church of England, and also that the Corporation should be empowered to reserve in each township such a portion of lands as might be sufficient to endow three or more parsonages if required. Among the advantages which, it was alleged, would result from the adoption of these proposals were these: That the Reserves would no longer be made a temptation to rebellion, by an invading enemy offering them to the lessees; that means would soon be afforded to multiply clergymen to any number required; and that a new link of attachment would be formed to the Mother Country. " Two hundred or three hundred clergymen (it was said), living in Upper Canada in the midst of their congregations, presented to their livings by the King, and receiving the greater part of their income from funds deposited in London, must attach the Province to the parent State; their influence would gradually spread; they would infuse into the population a tone and feeling entirely English, and acquiring by degrees the direction of education which the clergy at home have always possessed, the very first feelings, sentiments and opinions of the youth must become British." The real object of this new scheme, so ingeniously contrived and so plausibly commended, was evidently to place the control of the Clergy Reserves entirely in the hands of the Episcopal clergy. The scheme, however, was not sanctioned by Parliament, whose authorization was necessary to its being carried into effect; but arrangements were made by the British Government for selling part of the Clergy Reserves with the Crown Reserves to a company which was about to be established in 1824, and which was called the Canada Company. In consequence of these arrangements the Clergy Corporation received intimation that it was His Majesty's pleasure that they should be informed that it would be necessary for them to abstain from granting leases until further instructions were communicated.

Dr. Mountain, Bishop of Quebec, died in 1825, and a funeral sermon of an unusual character was preached on the occasion by Dr. Strachan, which was printed and "distributed among the members of His Majesty's Government by its author." The sermon contains a sketch of the history of the Church of England in Canada and an appeal to the British Government in its behalf. In pressing his appeal the preacher ventures to attack the ministers and preachers of other Churches, whose influence he represents as injurious to the Church and the political institutions of England. The following are extracts from this remarkable discourse: "The minister's influence is frequently broken or injured by numbers of uneducated itinerant preachers who, leaving their steady employment, betake themselves to preach the Gospel from idleness or a zeal without knowledge, by which they are induced, without any preparation, to teach what they do not know, and which from their pride they disdain to learn." "When it is considered that the religious teachers of the other denominations of Christians, a very few respectable ministers of the Church of Scotland excepted, come almost universally from the Republican States of America, where they gather their knowledge and form their sentiments, it is quite evident that if the Imperial Government does not immediately step forward with efficient help the mass of the population will be nurtured and instructed in hostility to our parent Church, nor will it be long till they imbibe opinions anything but favourable to the political institutions of England." This attack was specially aimed at the ministers of the Methodist Church, in whose behalf an indignant, eloquent and telling reply was written by the Rev. Egerton Ryerson, who had just entered on the work of the ministry as an itinerant Methodist preacher, and who did not hesitate to denounce the remarks made on the qualifications, motives and conduct of the Methodist preachers as "ungenerous, unfounded and false." With reference to this attack, as Mr. Ryerson afterwards wrote: "Up to this time, be it observed, not a word had been written respecting the Episcopal clergy or the Clergy Reserve question by any minister or member of the Methodist Church. At that time the Methodists had no law to secure a foot of land for parsonages, chapels and the burial of the dead; their ministers were not allowed to solemnise matrimony; and some of them had been the objects of cruel and illegal persecution on the part of magistrates and others in authority. And now were they the butt of unprovoked and unfounded aspersions from the heads of the Episcopal clergy, while pursuing the 'noiseless tenor of their way,' through trackless forests and bridgeless rivers, to preach among the scattered inhabitants the unsearchable riches of Christ."*

---

* Letters to Mr. Draper, 1838, pp. 14 and 15.

The subject of the Clergy Reserves was again brought before the Legislative Assembly in the session of 1825-26, and on the 27th January, 1826, an address to the King was adopted, in which the claims of Protestants of all denominations are advocated in the following terms:—
"We further most humbly represent, most gracious Sovereign, that the lands set apart in this Province for the maintenance and support of a Protestant clergy ought not to be enjoyed by any one denomination of Protestants, to the exclusion of their Christian brethren of other denominations equally conscientious in their respective modes of worshipping God, and equally entitled, as dutiful and loyal subjects, to the protection of your Majesty's benign and liberal Government; we therefore humbly hope it will, in your Majesty's wisdom, be deemed expedient and just that not only the present Reserves, but that any fund arising from the sales thereof, should be devoted to the advancement of the Christian religion generally and the happiness of all your Majesty's subjects, of whatever

denomination ; or, if such application should be deemed inexpedient, that the profits arising from such appropriation should be applied to the purposes of education and the general improvement of the province." To this address an unsatisfactory reply was transmitted on the 11th June, 1826. In this reply the Reserves are spoken of as "specially allotted by the Imperial Parliament to the 'Established Church.'"

It was felt, however, by the Imperial Government that something should be done for other Churches than that of England, but from other sources than the proceeds of the Clergy Reserves. From the funds, therefore, arising from the sales to the Canada Company allowances of £750 each were made to the Church of Scotland and the Roman Catholic Church, as appears from the following despatch, dated 6th October, 1826, from Earl Bathurst to Sir P. Maitland:—"Sir: You will receive instructions from the Treasury for the payment of £750 per annum for the salaries of the Presbyterian ministers, and a similar sum for the support of Roman Catholic priests. I deem it advisable that the allowances which may bo granted to ministers of the Presbyterian persuasion in Upper Canada should be limited to persons who are natural-born British subjects, who are in full communion with, and who are acknowledged by the Kirk of Scotland, by whom they should be recommended to the Lieutenant-Governor for their appointments. With respect to the Roman Catholic priests who are to receive an allowance from Government, they will be recommended to you by Bishop McDonnell, who will be considered responsible for their good conduct; and the Bishop himself, the Presbyterian ministers, and also the priests, should be required to produce your certificate that they have been in the active discharge of their duty for the period for which the salary is claimed, and that you have no objection to the payment being made." Payments to the ministers of the Church of Scotland in Upper Canada were first made in 1827.*

---

* Seventh Grievance Report, p. 168.

No provision was made at this time for the ministers of the United Presbytery, whose numbers were greater and the most of whom had laboured longer in the Province than the ministers of the Church of Scotland, and who therefore felt that an unjust discrimination had been made.

In the year 1826 the subject of the Clergy Reserves was again brought before the Legislative Assembly of Upper Canada and earnestly debated. The result was that on the 22nd December a series of resolutions was adopted by an overwhelming majority declaring that the exclusive "claim of the Protestant Episcopal Church is contrary to the spirit and meaning of the 31st Geo. III., and most injurious to the interests and wishes of the Province"; that but a comparatively small proportion of the inhabitants of Upper Canada are members of the Church of England, and ought not therefore to desire for their clergy the sole enjoyment of the Reserve lands, to the exclusion of their fellow-subjects, who were equally loyal to his Majesty's Government and the Constitution; that it is the

CHURCH AND STATE IN CANADA. 115

opinion of a great proportion of the people of the Province that the Clergy lands, in place of being enjoyed by the clergy of an inconsiderable part of the population, ought to be disposed of and the proceeds of their sale applied to increase the Provincial allowance for the support of district and common schools and the endowment of a Provincial seminary for learning, and in aid of erecting places of worship for all denominations of Christians. A Bill founded on these resolutions was passed by the Assembly in January, 1827, by a large majority, but it failed to obtain the assent of the Legislative Council.

While these proceedings were taking place in the Assembly, Dr. Strachan, now Archdeacon of York, was in England, to which he made a second journey, his object being at this time to secure the establishment and endowment of a university under the control of the Church of England. His efforts were successful; a royal charter was obtained for the University of King's College, with an endowment of 225,000 acres of land and a grant of £1,000 per annum for sixteen years. The provisions of the charter were sectarian in character. The bishop of the diocese was to be visitor; the president must be a clergyman of the Church of England; the college council was to consist of the chancellor, president and seven other members who were to be members of the Church of England, and who were required to sign the Articles of that Church: none were to be admitted to the degree of doctor of divinity but members of the Church of England. The establishment of this college was avowedly designed to place the education of the whole population of the Province under the control of the Church of England.*

At the time of Archdeacon Strachan's visit to England in the interests of King's College, a Bill was introduced into the House of Commons for the purpose of authorizing the sale and exchange of portions of the Clergy Reserves. During the

---

* See Macara's pamphlet on King's College, 1844, p. 16.

debate conflicting statements were made regarding the Churches of England and Scotland in Canada. On this occasion the Archdeacon wrote a letter, enclosing an ecclesiastical chart, to Mr. Horton, the Under-Secretary of the Colonial Department, which, he said, was intended to supply correct information respecting the state of the Churches in Upper Canada in 1827. The letter is dated 16th May, 1827, and gives a glowing description of the position and prospects of the Church of England as contrasted with those of the Church of Scotland, represents the Methodist ministers as exercising an influence hostile to British institutions, discusses the question of the Clergy Reserves, and gives a statement, similar to that previously made in the petition of the Clergy Corporation, of the advantages which would result from the adoption of the scheme they had proposed respecting the sale of the Clergy Reserves and the investment of the proceeds in England for the benefit of the Episcopal clergy. The following are extracts from this letter, which afterwards came into great notoriety:—

"I take the liberty of enclosing, for the information of Lord Goderich, an ecclesiastical chart of the Province of Upper Canada, which I believe to be correct, for the present year 1827, and from which it appears that the Church of England has made considerable progress, and is rapidly increasing.

"The people are coming forward in all directions offering to assist in building churches and soliciting with the greatest anxiety the establishment of a settled minister. Indeed the prospect of obtaining a respectable clergyman invites neighbourhoods together; and when one is sent of a mild, conciliatory disposition, he is sure in any settlement in which he may be placed to form the respectable part of the inhabitants into an increasing congregation. There are in the Province one hundred and fifty townships, containing forty to five hundred families, in each of which a clergyman may be most usefully employed, and double this number will be required in less than twelve years.

"When contrasted with other denominations

the Church of England need not be ashamed of the progress she has made. Till 1818 there was only one clergyman in Upper Canada a member of the Church of Scotland. This gentleman brought up his two sons in the Church of England, of which they are now parish priests. After his death his congregation was split into three divisions, which, with another collected at Kingston in 1822, count four congregations in all which are in communion with the Kirk of Scotland. Two are at present vacant, and of the two Scotch clergymen now in the Province one has applied for holy orders in the Church of England.

" The teachers of the different denominations, with the exception of the two ministers of the Church of Scotland, four Congregationalists and a respectable English missionary, who presides over a Wesleyan Methodist meeting at Kingston, are for the most part from the United States, where they gather their knowledge and form their sentiments. Indeed, the Methodist teachers are subject to the order of the Conference of the United States of America; and it is manifest that the Colonial Government neither has nor can have any other control over them, or prevent them from gradually rendering a large portion of the population, by their influence and instructions, hostile to our institutions, both civil and religious, than by increasing the number of the Established clergy.

"The Church of England in Canada was supported for many years out of the very limited and fluctuating revenue of the venerable Society for Propagating the Gospel in Foreign Parts, which did its utmost to increase the number of the clergy, but its means were so inadequate to the demand that it was at length obliged to solicit the aid of Government to continue and extend its efforts. Accordingly, a small sum in the aid of its funds has been for some years voted by the Imperial Parliament, of which Upper Canada receives a portion. How inefficient this aid is to supply the increasing necessities of the Colony has been sufficiently shown, for the tendency of the population is towards the Church of England, and nothing but the want of moderate means prevents her from spreading over the whole Province.

"But it may be asked: Why do not the Clergy Reserves afford a remedy?

"To make the answer to this question intelligible a few remarks are necessary.

"By the 31st George III., cap. 31, one-seventh of the land in Upper Canada is reserved for the maintenance of a Protestant clergy; the operation of which provision offers at this time the following results: The number of townships actually surveyed may be taken at 240, averaging 66,000 acres each, one-seventh of which, 9,428, equal forty-seven reserved lots of 200 acres each, consequently the number of such lots in 240 townships is almost 11,000, containing two and one-fifth millions of acres.

"But as these lands partake of the quality of those around them, many lots will be found, from various causes, unfit for cultivation, so that the number eligible for settlement cannot be taken at more than 9,000, containing 1,800,000 acres.

"That this provision will at no time be ample for the support of a religious establishment sufficient for the population of Upper Canada, when fully settled, will sufficiently appear from the fact that the whole surface of the Colony does not exceed 31,000,000 of acres, of which not more than 26,000,000 are capable of cultivation; one-seventh of this, containing 3,760,000 acres, or 18,800 reserved lots of 200 acres each, will ultimately constitute the whole property set apart for the maintenance of a Protestant clergy. Now, judging from what takes place in the United States, each lot will not produce in a century an average rent of £20 per annum, making a total of no more than £376,000, which, divided among two thousand clergymen (a very small number for a country nearly as large as England) gives only £188 to each."

In the Ecclesiastical Chart a list is given of thirty-one clergymen of the Church of England, which is called "the Established Church." A chaplain to the navy is included in the list, and also a Lutheran clergyman "under consideration." The names of Rev. Messrs. Johnston, Smart, Bell, McDowall, Harris and Jenkins are given as the "ministers of the Independent or Presbyterian order, and assuming the appellation of the Presbytery of the Canadas, but having no connection with the Kirk of Scotland." As "ministers in communion with the Kirk of Scotland" are given the names of the Rev. Messrs. McKenzie and McLaurin. In regard to the ministers of the Methodist and other Churches it is said: " As the Methodists have no settled clergymen, it has been found difficult to ascertain the number of itinerants employed, but it is presumed to be considerable—perhaps from twenty to thirty in the whole Province; one from England, settled at Kingston, appears to be a superior person. The other denominations have very few teachers, and these seemingly very ignorant."

The publication of the letter and chart in Canada produced great excitement and great indignation. Meetings were held, and numerous petitions were presented to the Legislative Assembly asking for an investigation of the statements made by Dr. Strachan, and also into the provisions of the charter of King's College. An investigation was accordingly made; a select committee, of which Mr. Marshall S. Bidwell was chairman, was appointed, and fifty-two witnesses, including members of the Council and Assembly, and clergymen of different denominations, were examined, and on their testimony a report was prepared and adopted by the Assembly by a majority of twenty-two to eight. According to the report "the letter and chart were calculated to produce, in many important respects, erroneous impressions respecting the religious state of this Province and the sentiments of its inhabitants." Allowance is made for the fact that, as stated in his evidence, they were drawn up by Dr. Strachan suddenly from memory, and without reference to sources of authentic information; but regret is expressed " that these circumstances had not been at least hinted in the letter itself, and the more so when it is considered that, as he stated to the committee, he had never known the number of members of the Church of England in this Province." The report of the select committee is valuable as giving information regarding the actual state of affairs in Canada, and the opinions entertained respecting the Clergy Reserves and the provisions of the university charter. The following are some of the particulars contained in it:—

In regard to the assertions in Dr. Strachan's letter that "the people are coming forward in all directions offering to assist in building churches, and soliciting with the greatest anxiety the establishment of a settled minister," and that "the tendency of the population is towards the Church of England, and nothing but the want of moderate support prevents her from spreading over the whole Province," the committee report that these are "completely contradicted by the evidence." On this subject the committee remark "that the Church of

England has always had in this Province peculiar advantages. It has been the religion of those high in office, and has been supported by their influence, and countenanced more than any other Church by the favour of the Executive Government. Its clergymen have had the exclusive right of marrying persons of all denominations indiscriminately: although by a Provincial statute the justices of the peace in General Quarter Sessions are empowered, if they shall deem it expedient, to authorise Lutheran and Calvinist clergymen and ministers of the Church of Scotland to marry any two persons of whom one has been for six months previously to such marriage a member of the congregation of the clergyman who performs the ceremony. This right the clergymen of the Church of England still exclusively enjoy, notwithstanding that the House of Assembly has for several sessions by a large majority passed a bill (which has not been concurred in by the honourable the Legislative Council) to extend this right to clergymen of Christian denominations in this

Province generally: the clergymen of the Church of England have also been liberally supported, and their churches partly or wholly built from the funds of a society in England. The solitary disadvantage mentioned by Dr. Strachan in his evidence before the committee of being obliged, for want of a bishop resident in the colonies, to resort to England for episcopal ordination, has never existed since the Province has had its present form of government—for during all that time a bishop has resided in Quebec. Still, the number of members of that Church has not increased in the same proportion as that of several other denominations. These facts confirm the opinion so generally expressed by the witnesses that the tendency of the population is not towards that Church. The contrary opinion, entertained by a few of the witnesses, may have arisen very naturally from a considerable increase in the number of missionaries of that Church, which, however, ought probably to be ascribed to the liberality with which salaries for their support are furnished by the Society for

Propagating the Gospel in Foreign Parts, rather than to any strong wish of the people to have clergymen of that Church settled among them." From the funds of this society "an annual salary is paid to every clergyman of the Church of England in this Province, in priest's orders, £200 sterling, and in deacon's orders, £100 sterling."

In regard to the Methodist ministers the committee thus vindicate their character: "The insinuations in the letter against Methodist clergymen the committee have noticed with peculiar regret. To the disinterested and indefatigable exertions of these pious men the Province owes much. At an early period of its history, when it was thinly settled, and its inhabitants were scattered through the wilderness and destitute of all other means of religious instruction, these ministers of the Gospel, animated by Christian zeal and benevolence, at the sacrifice of health and interest and comfort, carried among the people the blessings and consolations and sanctions of our holy religion. Their influence and instruction, far from having (as represented in the letter) a tendency hostile to our institutions, have been conducive, in a degree which cannot easily be estimated, to the reformation of their hearers from licentiousness and the diffusion of correct morals, the foundation of all sound loyalty and social order. There is no reason to believe that, as a body, they have failed to inculcate by precept and example, as a Christian duty, an attachment to the Sovereign and a cheerful and conscientious obedience to the laws of the country. More than thirty-five years have elapsed since they commenced their labours in the Colonies. In that time the Province has passed through a war which has put to the proof the loyalty of the people. If their influence and instructions have the tendency mentioned, the effects by this time must be manifest; yet no one doubts that the Methodists are as loyal as any of His Majesty's subjects."

With regard to the university charter the committee report some of its provisions, and add: "From the foregoing abstract of some of the provisions of the charter the sectarian character and tendency of the institution will be manifest. Dr. Strachan, by whose representations and exertions, in a great measure, the charter in its present shape seems to have been procured, in a pamphlet, published in London, entitled "An Appeal to the Friends of Religion and Literature in Behalf of the University of Upper Canada," distinctly states that it will be essentially a missionary college "for the education of missionaries of the Church of England"; and, as an argument to obtain from members of that Church contributions towards the funds of the college, maintains that the effect of establishing this university will be ultimately to make the greater portion of the population of the Province members of the Church of England. The opinions of the committee on the subject of a Provincial University are thus given: "It should not be a school of political or sectarian views. It should have about it no appearance of a spirit of partiality or exclusion. Its portals should be thrown open to all; and upon none who enter should any influence be exerted to attach them to a particular creed or church. It should be a source of intellectual and moral light and animation, from which the glorious irradiations of literature and science may descend upon all with equal lustre and power. Such an institution would be a blessing to the country, its pride and glory. Most deeply, therefore, is it to be lamented that the principles of the charter are calculated to defeat its usefulness, and to confine to a favoured few all its advantages."

The committee of Assembly's report was dated 15th March, 1828. In the previous week Archdeacon Strachan delivered a speech in the Legislative Council intended to repel the charges made against him with reference to his letter to Mr. Horton and the accompanying chart. On this occasion he furnished a new Ecclesiastical Chart for the year 1828. According to this chart there were, in 1828, in Upper Canada thirty-nine Episcopal ministers, six of the Church of Scotland, and twelve Presbyterian ministers not belonging to the Church of Scotland. A copy of the new chart was given to the committee, who with reference to it and other evidence respecting the number of ministers in the Province thus remark : " The chart furnished to the committee by Dr. Strachan, the evidence of the Rev. Egerton Ryerson, the evidence of Dr. Morrison, and the chart furnished by him, and generally the answers of the witnesses to the thirteenth and fourteenth questions, will enable the House to judge how far the Ecclesiastical Chart which accompanied Dr. Strachan's letter to Mr. Horton was a fair and accurate representation of the state of the different denominations of Christians in this Province." According to the chart prepared by Dr. Morrison the number of Methodist preachers was one hundred and seventeen,* and of Baptists forty-five, of Episcopalians thirty-one, of Presbyterians of the Church of Scotland six, of other Presbyterians sixteen,

---

* "Of these between forty and fifty were itinerants and the remainder local preachers. See Playter's History, p. 327.

CHURCH AND STATE IN CANADA. 133

of Mennonites and Dunkers twenty, of Wesleyan Methodists one.

An address to the King, founded on the committee's report, which was adopted by the Assembly, praying that the proceeds of the Clergy Reserves should be placed at the disposal of the Province for the purposes of general education and national improvement, was transmitted on the 10th May, 1828, by Governor Maitland in a despatch in which he ventures to assert that the charter of King's College was framed upon the most liberal principles, and in which he begs it to be distinctly understood that he gives not the slightest countenance to the statements and assumptions contained in the address respecting the Clergy Reserves and the Church of England. Soon afterwards Governor Maitland was appointed Lieutenant-Governor of Nova Scotia. During his ten years' tenure of office in Upper Canada he used every effort in favour of the exclusive claims of the Church of England.

Besides the address of the Legislative Assembly, numerously-signed petitions respecting the Clergy Reserves policy and other grievances were transmitted to England both from Upper and Lower Canada. A select committee was in consequence appointed by the House of Commons to investigate these matters. Witnesses, including clergymen and laymen from England, Scotland and Canada, were examined at length, and a report founded on their evidence was prepared by the committee. The report,* which is dated 12th July, 1828, expresses no doubtful opinion respecting the claims of the Church of Scotland to a share in the Clergy Reserves, and also respecting the intention of the framers of the Constitutional Act to reserve to the Government the right to apply the proceeds of the Reserves to "any Protestant clergy," as well as to endow with parsonages and glebes the clergy of the Church of England. The following is the language of the report: "The Act of 1791 directs that the profits arising from this source

---

* A copy of the report, evidence and petitions ordered by the House of Commons was republished in Quebec, in 1829, in a volume of three hundred and seventy-seven closely-printed pages, octavo.

shall be applied to a Protestant clergy; doubts have arisen whether the Act requires the Government to confine them to the use of the Church of England only or to allow the Church of Scotland to participate in them. The law officers of the Crown have given an opinion in favour of the rights of the Church of Scotland to such participation, in which your committee entirely concur; but the question has also been raised whether the clergy of every denomination of Christians, except Roman Catholics, may not be included; it is not for your committee to express an opinion on the accuracy which the words of the Act legally convey. They entertain no doubt, however, that the intention of those persons who brought forward the measure in Parliament was to endow with parsonage houses and glebe lands the clergy of the Church of England, at the discretion of the Local Government; but with respect to the distribution of the proceeds of the reserved lands generally they are of opinion that they sought to reserve to the Government the right to apply the money, if they so thought fit, to any Protestant clergy."

With reference to King's College the select committee advert to its sectarian character, and suggest changes in the following terms: "It cannot, they think, be doubted, as the guidance and government of the college is to be vested in the hands of the members of the Church of England, that in the election of professors a preference would inevitably be shown to persons of that persuasion; and in a country where only a small proportion of the inhabitants adhere to that Church a suspicion and jealousy of religious interference would necessarily be created.

"For these and other reasons the committee are desirous of stating their opinion that great benefit would accrue to the Province by changing the constitution of this body. They think that two theological professors should be established, one of the Church of England and another of the Church of Scotland, whose lectures the respective candidates for holy orders should be required to attend; but that with respect to the president, professors and all others connected with the college no religious test whatever should be required.

"That in the selection of professors no rule should be followed, and no other object sought than the nomination of the most learned and discreet persons, and that (with exception of the theological professors) they should be required to sign a declaration that, as far as it was necessary for them to advert to religious subjects, they would distinctly recognize the truth of the Christian revelation, but would abstain altogether from inculcating particular doctrines."

While the question of the Clergy Reserves occupied the attention of the Legislative Assembly of Upper Canada and the British House of Commons, it was discussed with great earnestness by the clerical representatives of the Churches in the Provinces. Thus we find the Bishop of Quebec addressing a letter, dated 6th December, 1827, to the clergy and congregations of his diocese, which then included the two Provinces, reiterating the arguments usually advanced in favour of the exclusive claims of the

Church of England; while in April, 1828, we find a pastoral letter,* signed by eleven clergymen of the Church of Scotland in Upper and Lower Canada, in which the Bishop's letter is reviewed, and the claims of the Church of Scotland reasserted and advocated at great length, and with not a little vehemence. In the pastoral letter allusion is made to the similar methods adopted in Scotland and Canada to force episcopacy on an unwilling people. By temptations addressed to ambition and covetousness, proselytes to prelacy, like Archbishop Sharpe, were secured in the time of the Stuarts, and these were the foremost in efforts to impose an uncongenial religion upon their country. So it is said in the pastoral letter: "Some features of resemblance may perhaps be discerned between the policy recommended and pursued in the days of Archbishop Sharpe and that which has been publicly avowed by the leaders of the Church

---

* Both letters are published in the first number of the *Canadian Miscellany*, April, 1828. This periodical continued to be published for only a few months.

of England in Upper and Lower Canada, and of these none is more remarkable than that Scotsmen and proselytes from presbytery to episcopacy should in both instances be the chief instruments."

Hitherto the claims of the ministers of the United Presbytery of Upper Canada, most of whom had come from the Irish and Scottish Secession Churches, had been very much disregarded, and they felt aggrieved that nothing had been granted or promised to them from public sources. They therefore, in September, 1829, presented a petition to Sir John Colborne, who had succeeded Sir P. Maitland as Lieutenant-Governor of Upper Canada, in which they urge their claims. They represent in their petition that they adhered to the doctrines and discipline of the Church of Scotland as contained in the Confession of Faith; that in Canada there were no real causes of separation between them and the Church of Scotland, with whom they were willing to unite; that although not united with that Church they had equal claims to public support; they were twelve in number, had laboured in the Province, some of them for thirty years, endeavouring to promote the spiritual and temporal welfare of the people, inculcating piety to God, loyalty to the King, and obedience to the laws; some of them preached in four or five different places, from twenty to thirty miles distant from each other; they had been educated in well-equipped seminaries of learning, and most of them had received degrees from the College of Glasgow. They therefore deemed themselves worthy to share in any provision which might be made for the support of Presbyterian ministers.

This petition was transmitted on the 25th January, 1830, by Governor Colborne to Sir George Murray, then principal Secretary of State for the Colonies, and who in reply wrote a despatch in which he said it was desirable that all the Presbyterian clergy of the Province should form one synod, and thus be placed on one footing with respect to any assistance the Government might grant for their support.

Copies of this despatch were sent to the ministers of the United Presbytery and the Church of Scotland. But about the time of its arrival the United Presbytery, not having received a reply to their petition to Governor Colborne, addressed another petition to Sir George Murray, in which they renew their claim to be placed on an equal footing with the ministers of the Church of Scotland. This petition was transmitted on the 4th September, 1830, by Sir John Colborne, who says: " I beg to state that, as the memorialists are some of the most diligent ministers in the Province, and have under their charge numerous congregations, it appears desirable for the interests of the large proportion of the population with whom they are connected that they should not be excluded from any future arrangements that may be made for the temporal support of the Presbyterian ministers.

We have now brought down the history of the Clergy Reserve controversy to the year 1831, and shall only add a few details respecting its future development and final settlement.

In 1836 the people of Canada were startled, and great indignation was manifested, by the discovery that in the beginning of the year—the 15th of January—Governor Colborne, in Council, had created forty-four rectories of the Church of England and endowed them with extensive and valuable glebe lands out of the Clergy Reserves. This was done in a clandestine manner, without the knowledge and in opposition to the declared policy of the Imperial Government, and also in direct opposition to the frequently repeated resolutions and declarations of the great majority of the representatives of the people of Upper Canada in the Legislative Assembly. This act of the Governor in Council was generally regarded as a breach of public faith, an unwarranted exercise of power, and a daring violation of the rights of the people, and was undoubtedly one of the chief causes of the rebellion of 1837-8. As the result of continued agitation, the Church of England was deprived in 1840 of an exclusive interest in the Clergy Reserves, while the claims of the Church of

CHURCH AND STATE IN CANADA. 143

Scotland and of other Churches were recognized. The Church of England, however, was permitted to retain a disproportionately large share of the proceeds of the Reserves. According to the Imperial Act of 7th August, 1840, it was arranged that while allowances to a limited extent should be made to other Churches, the remaining proceeds of the Clergy Reserve lands sold or to be sold should be divided into three parts, of which two were assigned to the Church of England and one to the Church of Scotland. This arrangement proved unsatisfactory, and agitation was renewed. The controversy was finally settled in 1854. In the previous year the Imperial Parliament authorized the Canadian Legislature to settle the question as it deemed best, with the provision "that it shall not be lawful for the said Legislature to *amend, suspend* or *reduce* any of the annual stipends or *allowances* which have already been given to the clergy of the Churches of England and Scotland, or to any other religious bodies or denominations of Christians in Canada (and to which the faith of the Crown is pledged), *during the natural lives of the parties now receiving the same."* Thus authorized, the Canadian Parliament passed an Act in 1854 by which the Clergy Reserves were finally alienated from religious to secular purposes. Liberal allowances were made to (the existing incumbents. The ministers of the Church of Scotland received upwards of five hundred thousand dollars, and those of the Church of England more than twice this amount ($1,113,770.02). The clergy (Ch. of Eng.) elected to commute, and after commutation to give their money to the Church, reserving a claim for interest or an annuity during their lives as secured by the Act referred to above. Consequently these moneys have been invested and made the basis of a permanent endowment for the ministers of these Churches. The Wesleyan Methodist Church received thirty-nine thousand and eighty-three dollars in commutation of its claims on the Clergy Reserves. Against the secularization of the Clergy Reserves Dr. Strachan, who had been appointed

Bishop of Toronto, protested and struggled with characteristic vigour, and with passionate and pathetic earnestness. Writing to the Duke of Newcastle, Secretary of State for the Colonies, he speaks of the anguish of his spirit in contemplating the spoliation of the Church of its vested rights by the Legislature of Canada, and declares that he would willingly avert, with the sacrifice of his life, the calamities which the passing of the Secularization Bill would bring upon the Church in Canada. He survived its passage for thirteen years,* during which it was his privilege to discover that his fears were groundless, and that the Church of England in Canada was stronger than before in true spiritual life and vigour.

Parliamentary records fail to furnish us with particulars as to the names and ages of the Presbyterian clergy who commuted; but Mr. James Croil, Treasurer of the Temporalities Fund of their Synod, dating from Morrisburg,

---

* He died in Toronto on the 1st November, 1867, in the ninetieth year of his age.

Ont., Dec. 1st, 1867, says: "Each of the ministers, during the year immediately preceding the commutation, had been in receipt of £150 per annum, and there were sixty-eight ministers on the roll who were recognized by Government and entitled to commutation. A calculation, based on their ages and probable lives, having been made, the result was that the sum of £127,448 2s. 10d. was placed to the credit of these sixty-eight ministers. (In sterling exchange, at $9\frac{1}{2}$ advance, this sum would be $620,247.05; in Halifax currency it would be £509,792.60)."

This money they agreed to invest in a common fund for the benefit of the Church in all time to come. They did more than this. Between the passing of the Imperial Act of 1853 and the Canadian Act of 1854 there had been added to the Roll of Synod eleven ministers; these were refused commutation by the Government, and it is evident that had the commuting ministers insisted on receiving each £150 annually from the fund, these eleven could receive nothing from it. The Synod regarded their claim as valid for commutation, but as the Government did not its members resolved to surrender £37 10s. per annum, accepting £112 10s. as their annual allowance in order that the others, hence known as "privileged ministers," might participate in the fund to the extent of, at least, £100 per annum. The Revs. Dr. Mathieson and Dr. Cook, and Messrs. John Thompson, Quebec, and Hugh Allen, Montreal, with the Hon. Thos. McKay, were appointed by the Synod in January, 1855, to effect the commutation and to manage the fund, and on the 4th of October following Dr. Cook reported that the negotiations had been completed on the terms just mentioned.

Many circumstances of arrangement and of public interest succeeded the final payment by the Government, all alike creditable to the financial abilities of the trustees and to the desire on the part of the members of the Synod to preserve order and unanimity of religious sentiment, but it is quite beyond the limits of time and space in this book to include them.

All we can say in concluding is, that for talent, natural and acquired, the first Presbyterian ministers who came from the Old and New World were distinguished ; their influence, though noiseless, was such as gives character and power to any country ; their hospitality was honest and sweetened all over with a vigorous and amiable expression; and their piety was made impressive by the instincts of gentlemen, and the display of that charity which thinketh no evil, but rejoiceth only in the truth.

CHAPTER VII.

Catholicism in London—Early Settlers—Early Difficulties—Progress and Voluntaryism—Quiet Patriotism—Correspondence.

"ARLY Days of Catholicism in London," is the heading of a quotation we make from "The City and Diocese of London," an engaging pamphlet replete with useful information. From it can be obtained a very fair apprehension of the progress made by Catholics in this part of Canada unaided by any thing but fidelity to their cause, and willing, cheerful hearts. Contrast the past with the present—voluntaryism, with the endowed pulpit from which have proceeded warnings since it first received preachers!

" The ecclesiastical history of London is not

less interesting than its political and municipal record. Some of the first settlers in the county of Middlesex were Irish and Scotch Catholics, so that while London was yet in the swaddling clothes of villagehood, there were Catholics to be found amongst its handful of inhabitants. The first church erected by the Catholics of Middlesex was built on the corner of Richmond Street and Maple Avenue, just opposite the Huron Hotel. The grounds around the church were used for a cemetery. The church itself was of the most primitive character, built of logs with an earthen floor. This modest place of worship was raised away back in the thirties, its dedication having taken place in 1834, the Rev. Father Downie, then stationed at St. Thomas, officiating. For many years there was no resident priest in London. At one time a whole year elapsed and no priest could visit the straggling mission by the Thames. Whenever a priest sent word that he was to come, Messrs. P. Smith, Dennis O'Brien,, James Reid, Hugh McCann, and Mr. Cruickshank, who were in these early days the leading Catholics in this neighbourhood, conveyed the glad message to the neighbours. The latter flocked into London on the day fixed for Mass, to seek reconciliation in the Holy Sacrament of Penance, and strength of soul in the Eucharistic Banquet. Then, too, many a Christian mother hastened into 'London town' to present her children to the minister of God to be born anew of water and of the Holy Ghost. Sometimes they met with bitter disappointment, for, occasionally, either the wretched condition of the roads or urgent calls to the sick or dying on the way, prevented the priest from reaching London at the time appointed."

These were the days of the best of good feeling among the settlers. No social distinctions were known, and every one seemed actuated by kindliness and charity towards his neighbour. Among the names of the pioneers of Catholicity in and about London are mentioned those of Garret Farrel, Patrick Smith, Dennis O'Brien, Capt. McLoughlin, A. McCausland, the Redmonds,

John Cruickshank, James Wilson, O'Byrne, P. McLoughlan, John Wright, John Walsh, O'Flynn, Flood, M. Kiely, P. McCann, John Orange, Peter Kennedy, Dr. Anderson, J. Martin, Jas. Reid, P. Burke, E. Burke, John Clegy, W. Darly, J. O'Brien, the Bruces, Andersons, Milnes, Johnstones, (Westminster); Dignam, Scanlan, P. Tierney, Charles and Matthew Colovin, E. Hillen, John M. Keary, Wm. Dalton, John Walsh, R. Dinahan, P. Cleary, Corbett, H. O'Brien and McLean. As late as the year 1850 there were not more than 200 Catholics in and about London, and yet between the years 1867 and 1884 to such an extent had they increased in wealth, numbers and devotion, that they were able to expend for church and educational work throughout the Diocese no less than $952,-798.

The separation of Church and State in Upper Canada is attributable entirely to the action of Protestant denominations. The Catholics had nothing to do with it, nor upon them could there be placed a distinguishing epithet on account of the prevalent disquietude over the Reserve Question.

The Rev. Dr. Ryerson, as we have already noticed, writes of them and says,—" My first remark is that this is a question agitated for more than twenty-five years, almost exclusively among Protestants in Canada, and the agitation of which, at the present time, has not in any way whatever been promoted by Roman Catholic influence. An attempt has been made in some quarters to create a contrary impression in England."

The first official record of the Roman Catholics, as a denomination, participating in the Clergy Reserves was in the year 1826, when an order was issued by the Treasury Department of the Provincial Executive of Upper Canada to pay out of the funds derived from the Canada Company £750 sterling a year for the salaries of Presbyterian ministers, and a like sum for Roman Catholic priests. The distribution of the money granted to the Roman Catholics was confided to Bishop McDonnell, who was invested with discretionary power to appropriate one-fourth of the annual grant to the support of schools. "With respect to the Roman Catholic priests," says Lord Bathurst in a despatch to Sir P. Maitland, dated October 6th, 1826, " who are to receive an allowance from Government, they will be recommended to you by Bishop McDonnell, *who will be responsible for their good conduct.*"

The next and the last we hear of the Roman Catholics in connection with the Clergy Reserve Question, is contained in the following official correspondence:—

KINGSTON, 9th July, 1855.

SIR,—Having been hitherto in the habit of receiving annually the Government allowance for the Catholic clergy of Upper Canada, as well as the five hundred pounds sterling allowed myself as Administrator Apostolic of the Diocese of Kingston, I have the honour to inform you that I wish to avail myself of the benefit of the Commutation Clause under the terms of the Act passed in the Provincial Parliament on the 18th December last, and therefore shall immediately transmit a power of attorney to the Very Rev. C. F. Cazeau, Vicar-General at Quebec, whom I have appointed my Attorney *ad hoc*. I therefore respectfully request that you will as soon as possible effect a commutation of the above in my favor, together with such a portion of the arrears as might be due to the aforesaid Catholic clergy since the year 1840.

I have the honor, &c.
Signed, † PATRICK PHELAN,
Bishop of Carrhoe,
Administrator Apostolic,
Diocese of Kingston.
The Honourable
The PROVINCIAL SECRETARY.

SECRETARY'S OFFICE,
QUEBEC, 8th August, 1855.

MY LORD,—I have the honour, by command of His Excellency the Governor-General, to inform you that His Excellency has under his consideration in Council your letter of the 9th ultimo, requesting that the Government allowance to the Roman Catholic clergy of Upper Canada, £1,000 sterling, as well as your own allowance as Administrator of the Diocese of Kingston,

£500 sterling, should be commuted under the provisions of the recent Clergy Reserve Act.

His Excellency in Council has been pleased to direct that the aggregate of the two sums above mentioned, viz., £1,500 sterling, should be commuted for £20,932 15s. currency, that being the value of such sum for 20 years, the interest being taken at six per cent. per annum.

His Excellency in Council has further been pleased to direct that debentures for the last mentioned sum be issued to be charged on the Clergy Reserve Fund of Upper Canada, and that the commutation take place from 1st July last.

I have, &c.,
Signed, G. E. CARTIER, *Secretary.*
The Right Reverend
The Roman Catholic
Bishop of Kingston, C. W.

ARCHIEPISCOPAL PALACE, QUEBEC,
25th September, 1855.

SIR,—I hold a power of attorney from Monseigneur Phelan, Bishop of Carrhoe, Administrator of the Diocese of Kingston, under which I am authorized to settle with the Government the commutation of that part of the Clergy Reserves which falls to the share of the Catholic clergy of Upper Canada in conformity with the Act 17 and 18 Vic., cap. 2.

A proposal was recently made to me, that I should receive the amount of the commutation in question (£20,932 15s. currency) in Government debentures bearing interest at six per cent., at a premium of $14\frac{1}{2}$ per cent.

Inasmuch as these debentures can nowhere be negotiated with advantage, but at London, and as the negotiation of them would entail great trouble, the Bishop of Carrhoe, who has but small leisure to devote to such business, is desirous of receiving the amount in question in cash rather than in debentures.

I think it a duty incumbent on me to communicate to you the wish of that prelate, and I flatter myself that His Excellency the Governor-General will graciously take it into his favourable consideration.

I have the honour to be, &c.
Signed, C. F. CAZEAU, V.G.
The Honourable
GEO. E. CARTIER,
Provincial Secretary.

SECRETARY'S OFFICE,
QUEBEC, 1st October, 1855.

REV. SIR,—I am commanded by His Excellency the Governor-General to inform you that he has had under his consideration in Council your letter of the 25th ult., requesting, on behalf of His Lordship the Roman Catholic Bishop of Carrhoe, the Administrator of the Diocese of Kingston, that the amount of commutation payable to the Roman Catholic clergy of Upper Canada out of the Clergy Reserve Fund, viz., £20,932 15s. currency, be paid not in debentures but in money.

His Excellency in Council has been pleased to accede to the request of His Lordship, and has directed that payment of one-half of the said amount be made on the 1st January next, and the other half on the 1st July, 1856, with interest at the rate of six per cent. per annum, from 1st July next.

I have, &c.,
G. E. CARTIER, *Secretary.*
The Rev. C. F. CAZEAU, V.G.

CHAPTER VIII.

Early Excitement—Imperial Legislation—Existing Interests Guaranteed—A Protest—Canadian Legislation and Protection—Bishop Strachan—The Clergy Influenced—The Hon. J. H. Cameron—Table Showing who Commuted—Blending of Church and State.

E now arrive at an important period—1854-55—not only for the Church of England people, but for all the denominations of Upper Canada. In 1817-19 this reserve property first attracted the attention of the Colonial Legislature. Agitation, the rebellion of 1837-38, petitions, counter petitions, and protests followed along in succession until 1853, when an Act passed the Imperial Parliament authorizing the Canadian Legislature in these terms:

"To vary or repeal all or any of the existing provisions of the Reserve Fund, and to apply the proceeds to any purpose they might see fit; provided, that it shall not be lawful for the said Legislature to *amend, suspend, or reduce any of the annual stipends or allowances* which have already been given to the clergy of the Churches of England and Scotland, or to any other religious bodies or denominations of Christians in Canada (and to which the faith of the Crown is pledged), *during the natural lives* or incumbencies of the parties now receiving the same."

This Act naturally threw the Bishop (Strachan) and his adherents into a fearful commotion; and at a meeting of the Synod in 1854, a vigorous protest was adopted as follows :—

"The Lord Bishop, Clergy, and Lay Delegates of the United Church of England and Ireland, in the Province of Canada West, in Synod duly assembled at Toronto, on Thursday, the 26th day of October, A.D. 1854, hereby solemnly protest against the enactment of a certain measure now before the Legislative Assembly of this Province, having for its avowed object to dispossess the said Church and other religious bodies in this Province, of all the right and title to the benefit and proceeds arising out of the lands formerly set apart by the Crown for the support of the Protestant clergy, and which benefit and proceeds were still further guaranteed by the Imperial Act of 1840."

The commotion and protest proved abortive. By an Act in accord with the Imperial one, the Clergy Reserves were handed over for secular purposes to the municipal corporations, provision being made to satisfy the claims of the existing incumbents, whose *annual stipends or allowances* the Governor-in-Council was empowered to commute, according to the following clause:—

"Be it therefore enacted, that the Governor in Council may, whenever he may deem it expedient, with the consent of the parties and bodies severally interested, commute with the said parties such annual stipends or allowances thereof, to be calculated at the rate of 6 per cent. per annum, upon the probable life of each individual, and, in case of the bodies specified (namely, the Churches of England and Scotland, and others to whom the faith of the Crown is pledged), at the actual value of the said allowances received at the time of commutation, to be calculated at the rate aforesaid."

The clergy of the Church of England were informed, and correctly so, that if they commuted at all it must be effected within one year from the passing of the Act. They were appealed to in many ways to give authority to some attorney to transact the business and receive the money for them.

Scotch character is filled with meditative and disciplinary qualities not in harmony with the loose reins of Quixotic cynicism. From birth to manhood the Bishop had been of this class, and he was never in better humour than when engaged in constructive exercises. He having at an early date been a school teacher, judges, lawyers, clerics and merchants had emerged from his tuition as pupils do from a mercantile college at the present day.

Every one acquainted with a distinguished dinner party of gray-headed officials assembled at his "Palace"—now a large, old-fashioned, brick boarding house on Front Street, Toronto—will

CHURCH AND STATE IN CANADA. 163

recollect his manner of summoning his guests to the banqueting table. Opening the door his grotesque voice, in a dialect he could never surrender, was recognized in: "Boys, come to dinner." Obedience was a rule easily observed at such an event. Nor was it less observed when the Clergy Reserve repast was prepared as viands for a large reception.

In preparation for it the Bishop wrote letters to the clergy, couched in persuasive and almost peremptory instructions as to what they might, could, would, or should do in the premises. He sent commissioners to them who, by every possible representation, backed up a pastoral letter, dated 20th January, 1855, wherein he *urged them* on five different grounds to commute their claims to the Clergy Reserve Funds. He gave the clergy a guarantee that their *individual claims* to a stipend *would be secured to them* by the Church *during their natural lives*. (*Canons, By-Laws, etc., Diocese of Toronto, 1851-1872*, p. 144.) So, partly by persuasion, partly by magisterial influence and Episcopal authority, he gained the signatures of the young and inexperienced clergy; while to the older and rectorial ones, as subsequent events narrated, there were held up for hopeful vision archidiaconal, ruridecanal, canonical, and other official parchments illuminated with a large red Episcopal seal.

Anticipated accessions of salary, after specified removals of then living prebendaries, also adorned the parchments as tassels to a banner.

To the Hon. John Hillyard Cameron, Q.C., M.P.P., were given powers of attorney; and on the strength of them, according to statute, the Receiver-General verified Mr. Cameron's exhibit of those entitled to, and who consented to commute and give the proceeds to the Church, instead of putting it in their own pockets, as they might have done, or not to commute at all, leaving the capital to fall into the hands of the Government at the time of their death, and after receiving to such a time the usual State allowance. Those who did not commute have either no sums following their names, or their names are omitted altogether.

Here is a copy of the authenticated list:—

CHURCH AND STATE IN CANADA. 165

LIST OF THE CLERGY in the Diocese of Toronto drawing from the Clergy Reserve Fund in Upper Canada, as approved by the Lord Bishop of Toronto, on the 1st of March, 1855, claiming and entitled to commute their annual stipend for the value thereof, according to the provisions of the Provincial Act 17 and 18 Victoria, to make better provision for the appropriation of monies arising from the lands known as the Clergy Reserves.

NAMES OF CLERGY.	Stipend.			Age.	Expecta- tions of Life.	Present Value.	Total. Sterling.			Dols. and Cts.
	£	s.	d.		YEARS	YEARS	£	s.	d.	$ cts.
T Alexander, Rev. J. L.....	136	17	6	53	18.97	11.15	1526	3	1½	7427 29
T Allen, Rev. Thos. W.....	100	0	0	33	32.36	14.15	1415	0	0	6886 34
O Anderson, Rev. Gus. A..	120	0	0	29	35.00	14.49	1738	16	0	8462 16
T Ardagh, Rev. S. B.......	121	13	4	51	20.39	11.56	1406	9	4	6844 81
T Armstrong, Rev. J. Gilbert	100	0	0	29	35.00	14.49	1449	0	0	7051 81
T Atkinson, Rev. A. F.	206	16	8	51	20.39	11.56	2390	19	10	11636 16
T Atkinson, Rev. A. F.	18	5	0				210	19	5	1026 73
T Baker, Rev. E...........	0	0	0	28			0	0	0	0 00
Braven, Rev. James......	0	0	0	53			0	0	0	0 00
T Beck, Rev. J. Walton....	100	0	0	26	37.14	14.75	1475	0	0	7178 34
T Belt, Rev. William	120	0	0	28	35.69	14.58	1749	12	0	8514 73

LIST OF THE CLERGY in the Diocese of Toronto—Continued.

NAMES OF CLERGY.	Stipend.			Age.	Expecta-tions of Life.	Present Value.	Total Sterling.			Dols. and Cts.	
	£	s.	d.		YEARS	YEARS	£	s.	d.	$	cts.
T Bethune, Ven. A. H.	206	16	8	54	18.28	10.94	6255	17	2	30445	21
T Bethune, Ven. A. H.	365	0	0							6479	16
T Bethune, Ven. A. H.	121	13	4				1331	6	8	5117	30
H Bettridge, Ven. Wm.	121	13	4	63	12.81	8.64	1051	4	0	0	00
T Blackman, Rev. T. J. M. W.	0	0	0	25			0	0	0	12250	19
Blake, Rev. D. E.	206	16	8	48	22.51	12.17	2517	3	3	8696	92
O Blakey, Rev. Robert	206	16	8	63	12.81	8.64	1787	0	9	8106	00
O Bleasdell, Rev. Wm.	121	13	4	37	29.64	13.69	1665	12	4	7466	52
H Boomer, Rev. Michael	121	13	4	45	24.46	12.61	1534	4	4	10730	24
O Boswell, Rev. E. J.	206	16	8	55	17.58	10.66	2204	16	10	7011	80
O Boustield, Rev. Thomas	100	0	0	29	35.00	14.49	1449	0	0	6925	27
O Bower, Rev. E. C.	100	0	0	32	33.03	14.23	1423	0	0	6662	47
T Brent, Rev. Henry	100	0	0	37	29.64	13.69	1369	0	0	5690	19
H Brough, Rev. C. C.	121	13	4	59	14.92	9.61	1169	4	4	6808	94
H Brown, Rev. Charles	100	0	0	38	28.96	13.58	1358	0	0	3589	17
T Bull, Rev. Geo. A.	50	0	0	26	37.14	14.75	737	10	0	11867	66
T Burnham, Rev. Mark	206	16	8	50	21.11	11.79	2438	11	3	8633	00
T Baldwin, Rev. Edmund	121	13	4	28	35.69	14.58	1773	18	0	6157	96
H Campbell, Rev. R. F.	121	13	4	56	16.89	10.40	1265	6	0	0	00
Campbell, Rev. Thos. S.	0	0	0	23			0	0	0		

CHURCH AND STATE IN CANADA. 167

Name											
Carroll, Rev. John	0	0	0	26			0	0	0	0	00
H Caulfield, Rev. A. St. G.	121	13	4	31	33.68	14.32	1742	5	4	8479	00
T Cooper, Rev. H. C.	121	13	4	48	22.57	12.17	1480	13	8	6816	66
O Coy, Rev. R. G.	100	0	0	31	31.68	13.98	1398	0	0	6803	60
T Clark, Rev. J. S.	120	0	0	48	22.51	12.17	1460	8	0	7127	29
O Clark, Rev. W. C.	120	0	0	44	25.09	12.80	1536	0	0	7425	20
T Creen, Rev. Thomas	206	16	8	55	17.58	10.66	2204	15	10	10730	00
H Cronyn, Rev. Ben.	206	16	8	52	19.68	11.33	2343	8	5	11404	66
T Darling, Rev. W. Stewart	121	13	4	36	30.32	13.81	1680	4	4	8177	05
T Denroche, Rev. Edward	206	16	8	51	20.39	11.56	2390	19	10	11636	16
H Dewar, Rev. E. H.	120	0	0	42	26.34	13 06	1567	4	0	7997	04
T Dixon, Rev. Alex.	100	0	0	34	31.68	13.98	1298	0	0	6803	60
Dobbs, Rev. F. W.	0	0	0	39			0	0	0	0	00
H Elliot, Rev. F. Gore	121	13	4	40	27.61	13.32	1620	12	0	7884	24
H Ellwood, Rev. E. L.	150	0	0	44	25.09	12.80	1920	0	0	9344	00
H Evans, Rev. Francis	206	16	8	53	18.97	11.15	2306	3	10	11223	47
H Faquier, Rev. F. D.	100	0	0	37	29.64	13.69	1369	0	0	6662	47
T Fletcher, Rev. John	100	0	0	39	28.28	13.45	1345	0	0	6545	67
T Flood, Rev. John	121	13	4	42	26.34	13.06	1588	19	4	7732	97
H Flood, Rev. Richard	121	13	4	60	14.34	9.43	1147	6	4	5583	61
T Fuller, Rev. Thos. B.	121	13	4	44	25.09	12.80	1557	6	8	7579	02
T Garrett, Rev. Richard	121	13	4	42	26.34	13.06	1588	19	4	7732	97
H Gibson, Rev. Jos. C.	40	0	0	24	38.59	14 90	596	0	0	2900	53
T Geddes, Rev. J. G.	121	13	4	43	25.71	12.88	1567	1	4	7626	39
T Givens, Rev. Saltern	206	16	8	46	23.82	12.50	2585	8	0	12582	37
O Godfrey, Rev. James	100	0	0	30	34.31	14.40	1440	0	0	7008	01
T Grasett, Rev. Elliot	100	0	0	29	35.00	14.49	1449	0	0	7051	81
T Green, Rev. Thomas	121	13	4	45	24.46	12.61	1534	4	4	7446	32

168   HISTORY OF THE SEPARATION OF

LIST OF THE CLERGY in the Diocese of Toronto—Continued.

NAMES OF CLERGY.	Stipend.			Age.	Expecta- tions of Life.	Present Value.	Total. Sterling.			Dols. and Cts.
	£	s.	d.		YEARS	YEARS	£	s.	d.	$ cts.
o Grier, Rev. John	206	16	8	64	12.30	8.50	1758	1	8	8556 01
o Greig, Rev. William	121	13	4	45	24.46	12.61	1534	4	4	7466 52
o Groves, Rev. T. P. S.	100	0	0	43	25.71	12.88	1288	0	0	6268 28
II Gunne, Rev. John	100	0	0	40	27.61	13.32	1332	0	0	6482 40
o Harris, Rev. Michael	121	13	4	60	14.34	9.43	1147	6	4	5583 61
o Harris, Rev. James	100	0	0	33	32.36	14.15	1415	0	0	6886 34
T Hallen, Rev. George	121	13	4	60	14.34	9.43	1147	6	4	5583 61
T Harding, Rev. Robert	121	13	4	47	23.17	12.33	1500	3	0	7300 73
o Harper, Rev. W. F. S.	121	13	4	45	24.46	12.61	1534	4	4	7465 55
Hayward, Rev. Henry	0	0	0	34			0	0	0	0 00
T Hickie, Rev. John	100	0	0	46	23.82	12.50	1250	0	0	6083 34
T Hill, Rev. Arthur	100	0	0	30	34.34	14.40	1440	0	0	7008 01
T Hill, Rev. Geo. S. F.	121	13	4	34	31.68	13.98	1700	18	0	8277 72
T Hill, Rev. Bold C.	121	13	4	55	17.58	10.66	1296	19	4	8311 91
T Hilton, Rev. John	50	0	0	34	31.68	13.98	596	0	0	2900 53
Hebden, Rev. John	0	0	0	38			0	0	0	0 00
II Holland, Rev. Henry*	100	0	0	36	30.32	13.81	1381	0	0	6720 87
Inglis. Rev. Charles L.	0	0	0	32			0	0	0	0 00

* Supplementary Cheque given to make £120.

CHURCH AND STATE IN CANADA. 169

	Name									
H	Jamieson, Rev. Andrew*	121	13	4	40	27.61	13.32	1620	12	0	7896	92
H	Jessopp, Rev. Henry B.*	80	0	0	28	35.69	14.58	1166	8	0	7136	49
H	Johnson, Rev. C. Campbell	30	0	0	26	37.14	14.75	442	10	0	2153	50
	Johnson, Rev. W. A.	0	0	0	39			0	0	4	0	00
T	Kennedy, Rev. Thos. S.	171	13	14	39	28.28	13.45	2308	18	0	11236	73
H	Kennedy, Rev. John	120	0	0	35	31.00	13.92	1670	8	4	8129	29
O	Kerr, Rev. Matthew	121	13	4	43	25.91	12.88	1567	1	0	7626	39
	Langtry, Rev. John	0	0	0	23			0	0	0	0	00
H	Lampman, Rev. Archd.	120	0	0	32	33.3	14.23	1707	12	0	8310	33
O	Lauder, Rev. W. B.	150	0	0	36	30.32	13.81	2071	10	0	10081	30
O	Lauder, Rev. John S	100	0	0	25	37.86	14.82	1482	0	0	7212	41
T	Leeming, Rev. Wm.	206	16	8	67	10.73	7.76	1605	0	6	7811	12
T	Leeming, Rev. Ralph	121	13	4	66	11.27	8.2	975	15	4	4748	73
T	Lett, Rev. Stephen	150	0	0	40	27.61	13.32	1998	0	0	9643	60
O	Lewis, Rev. J. Travers	150	0	0	29	35.00	14.49	2173	10	0	10577	71
	Lewis, Rev. Richard	120	0	0	31	33.68	14.32	1718	9	0	8361	10
	Lewis, Rev. D.	0	0	0	26			0	0	0	0	00
T	Logan, Rev. William	100	0	0	31	33.68	14.32	1432	0	0	6969	07
T	Lundy, Rev. F. J.	150	0	0	40	27.61	13.32	1998	0	0	9643	60
	Leach, Rev. Thomas	0	0	0	26			0	0	0	0	00
	Macaulay, Rev. Wm.	0	0	4	55	17.58	10 66	1296	19	4	6311	95
H	Mack, Rev. Frederick	121	13	4	44	25.09	12 80	1557	8	8	7579	52
T	McMurray, Rev. Wm.	121	13	4	32	33.03	14.23	1423	0	0	6925	27
T	McKenzie, Rev. J. G. D.	100	0	0	44	25.09	12 80	1280	0	0	6230	56
T	McNab, Rev. Alex.	100	0	0	39	28.28	13.45	1345	5	0	6545	67
H	Marsh, Rev. John W.	100	0	0	32	33.03	14.23	1707	12	0	8310	33
T	Marsh, Rev. Thos. W.	120	0	0	41	26.97	13.21	1607	4	4	7821	79
T	McGeorge, Rev. R. J.	121	13									

* Supplementary Cheque given to make £120.

LIST OF THE CLERGY in the Diocese of Toronto—Continued.

NAMES OF CLERGY.	Stipend.			Age.	Expectations of Life.	Present Value.	Total Sterling.			Dols. and Cts.
	£	s.	d.		YEARS	YEARS	£	s.	d.	$ cts.
T Mayerhoffer, Rev. R.	73	0	0	70	6.80	6.80	496	8	0	2415 82
T Mitchell, Rev. Richard	150	0	0	35	31.00	13.92	2088	0	0	10161 61
O Morris, Rev. E.	121	13	4	49	21.81	11.90	1447	16	8	7046 12
O Morris, Rev. J. A.	55	0	0	30	34.34	14.40	792	0	0	3854 40
H Mortimer, Rev. Arthur	121	13	4	39	28.28	13.45	1636	8	0	7963 80
H Mulholland, Rev. A. H. R.	100	0	0	30	34.34	14.40	1440	0	0	7008 01
O Mulock, Rev. John A.	100	0	0	40	27.61	13.32	1332	0	0	6482 40
T Merritt, Rev. R. N.	100	0	0	28	35.69	14.58	1458	0	0	7095 61
H Mockridge, Rev. James	121	13	4	39	28.34	13.45	1636	8	0	7963 90
T Osler, Rev. F. L.	182	10	0	49	21.81	11.90	2171	15	0	10569 19
T Osler, Rev. Henry Y.	121	13	4	39	28.28	13.45	1636	8	0	7963 90
H Padfield, Rev. James	121	13	4	52	19.68	11.33	1378	9	0	6678 62
T Palmer, Rev. Arthur	206	16	8	48	22.50	12.17	2517	3	3	12250 17
O Patton, Rev. Henry	206	16	8	48	22.51	12.17	2517	3	3	12250 17
H Paterson, Rev. Ephraim	100	0	0	28	35.69	14.58	1458	0	0	7095 61
T Pentland, Rev. John	121	13	4	50	21.11	11.79	1434	9	0	6981 00
O Pettit, Rev. Charles Y.	100	0	0	28	35.69	14.58	1458	0	0	7095 61
T Phillips, Rev. H. N.	50	0	0	49	21.81	11.90	595	0	0	2895 67
O Plees, Rev. H. F.	100	0	0	34	31.68	13.98	1398	0	0	6803 60
O Pyne, Rev. Alexander	121	13	4	37	29.64	13.69	1665	12	4	8103 00

CHURCH AND STATE IN CANADA.

Name	£	s.	d.	No.				£	s.	d.	£	s.	d.
Preston, Rev. James A.	0	0	0				0	0	0	0	0	0	00
T Ramsay, Rev. S. F.	150	0	0	23			1825	0	0	0	8884	10
T Read, Rev. Thomas B.	121	13	4	48	22.51	12.17	1652	13	9	4	8040	89
H Revell, Rev. Henry	121	13	4	38	28.96	13.58	1169	13	4	4	5690	19
T Ritchie, Rev. William	121	13	4	59	14.92	9.61	1296	13	19	0	6311	91
Robarts, Rev. Thomas	0	0	0	55	17.58	10.66	0	0	0	0	0	00
o Rogers, Rev. R. V.	121	13	4	23	20.39	11.56	1406	13	9	4	6844	81
o Rolph, Rev. Romaine	206	16	0	51	14.92	9.61	1987	16	13	8	9733	42
o Rothwell, Rev. John	121	13	4	59	16.89	10.40	1265	13	6	0	6157	96
o Ruttan, Rev. Charles	121	13	4	56	32.36	14.15	1721	13	11	8	8431	23
H Salter, Rev. J. G. R.	121	13	4	33	28.28	13.45	1636	13	8	0	7962	05
T Sanson, Rev. Alex.	121	13	4	39	30.32	13.81	1680	13	4	0	8177	05
H Sandys, Rev. F.	150	0	0	36	35.00	14.49	2173	16	10	0	10577	71
T Scadding, Rev. Henry	60	16	8	29	26.97	13.21	803	0	12	0	3910	89
Stennett, Rev. Walter	0	0	0	41			0	0	0	0	0	00
o Shirley, Rev. Paul	121	13	4	33	14.92	9.61	1169	13	4	4	5690	19
T Shanklin, Rev. Robert	100	0	0	59	33.03	14.23	1423	13	0	0	6925	27
T Shortt, Rev. Jonathan	121	13	4	32	24.66	12.61	1534	0	0	0	7466	52
Smyth, Rev. James	0	0	0	45			0	0	0	0	0	00
T Smithurst, Rev. J.	100	0	0	28	23.17	12.33	1233	0	8	0	6000	61
o Stephenson, Rev. R. L.	91	5	0	47	35.69	14.58	1130	0	0	0	5499	34
H Stimson, Rev. E. R.	100	0	0	28	34.34	14.40	1440	0	0	0	7008	00
T Stewart, Rev. E. M.	30	0	0	30	16.21	10.18	354	0	0	0	1722	80
o Strong, Rev. S. S.	0	0	0	57	18.97	11.15	1356	13	11	8	6602	04
o Stuart, Ven. G. O.	121	13	4	53								
‡ o Stuart, Ven. G. O.												
Stuart, Ven. G. O.	693	10	0	78	6.82	4 99	3460	10	11	4	16840	76
H Street, Rev. ———	121	13	4	41	26.97	13.21	1607	13	4	4	7821	79

LIST OF THE CLERGY in the Diocese of Toronto—Continued.

NAMES OF CLERGY.	Stipend.			Age.	Expectations of Life.	Present Value.	Total Sterling.			Dols. and Cts.
	£	s.	d.		YEARS	YEARS	£	s.	d.	$ cts.
o Tooke, Rev. J. Reynolds..	100	0	0	30	34.34	14.40	1440	0	0	7008 01
H Townley, Rev. Adam	121	13	4	47	23.17	12.33	1500	3	0	7300 73
o Trenayne, Rev. F. S.	75	0	0	58	15.55	9.93	744	15	0	3624 45
T Toronto, Lord Bishop of.	1520	16	8	76	6.69	5.30	8060	8	4	38933 36
H Usher, Rev. J. C.	121	13	4	46	23.82	12.50	1520	16	8	7401 15
H Van Linge, Rev. J.	120	0	0	41	26.97	13.21	1585	4	0	7714 64
o Watkins, Rev. N.	60	0	0	48	22.51	12.17	730	4	9	3553 49
T Wilson, Rev. John	121	13	4	47	23.17	12.33	1500	3	0	7303 03
o Worrell, Rev. John B. ...	100	0	0	33	32.36	14.15	1415	0	0	6886 34
	£19,208	0	10				£227,995	2	4½	$1,113,770 02

Sterling Exchange at 9½ per cent. advance Par.

TORONTO, 20th June, 1855.

(Signed), J. HILLYARD CAMERON.

N.B.—The names having (H) are those of Clergymen whose capital went to the Diocese of Huron. Those having (T) to the Diocese of Toronto. Those having (o) to the Diocese of Ontario. The recipients at the time of the Commutation being residents within the limits of the Dioceses respectively.

CHURCH AND STATE IN CANADA.   173

AUTHENTICATED LIST OF CLERGY in the present Diocese of Huron who drew upon the Clergy Reserve Fund in Upper Canada, as approved by the Lord Bishop of Toronto, on the 1st of March, 1855, claiming and entitled to commute their annual stipends for the value thereof, according to the provisions of the Provincial Act 17 and 18 Victoria, to make better provision for the appropriation of monies arising from the lands known as the Clergy Reserves.

NAMES OF CLERGY.	Pounds.			Commutation. Pounds Sterling.			Age.	Reduced to Dollars and Cents.	
	£	s.	d.	£	s.	d.		$	cts.
Beltridge, Rev. William.......	121	13	4	1051	4	0	63	5117	30
Boomer, Rev. Michael........	121	13	4	1534	4	4	45	7466	52
Brough, Rev. C. L............	121	13	4	1169	4	4	59	5690	16
Brown, Rev. C.	100	0	0	1358	0	8	38	6808	94
Campbell, Rev. R. F..........	121	13	4	1265	6	4	56	6157	96
Caulfield, Rev. A. St. G.	121	13	4	1742	5	4	31	8479	00
Cronyn, Rt. Rev. B...........	206	16	8	2343	8	0	52	11404	66
Dewar, Rev. E. H.............	120	0	0	1567	4	0	42	7997	04
Elliot, Rev. F. G..............	121	13	4	1620	12	0	40	7884	24
Ellwood, Rev. E. L.	150	0	0	1920	0	0	44	9344	00
Evans, Rev. F.................	206	16	8	2306	3	10	53	11223	47
Flood, Rev. Richard	121	13	4	1147	6	4	60	5583	61
Gibson, Rev. J. C.	40	0	0	596	0	0	24	2900	53
Gunne, Rev. F. M.	100	0	0	1332	0	0	40	6482	40

AUTHENTICATED LIST OF CLERGY in the present Diocese of Huron—Continued.

NAMES OF CLERGY.	Pounds.			Commutation. Pounds Sterling.			Age.	Reduced to Dollars and Cents.
	£	s.	d.	£	s.	d.		$ cts.
Holland, Rev. Henry*	100	0	0	1381	0	0	36	6720 87
Jamieson, Rev. A.	121	13	4	1620	12	0	40	7886 92
Jessopp, Rev. H. B.*	80	0	0	1166	8	0		7136 49
Johnson, Rev. C. C.*	30	0	0	442	10	0	26	2153 50
Kennedy, Rev. John	120	0	0	1670	8	0	35	8129 29
Laupman, Rev. Archd.	120	0	0	1707	12	0	32	8310 33
Mack, Rev. Frederick	121	13	4	1296	19	4	55	6311 95
Marsh, Rev. J. W.	100	0	0	1345	0	0	39	6545 67
Mortimer, Rev. A.	121	13	4	1636	8	4	39	7963 80
Mockridge, Rev. James	121	13	4	1636	8	4	39	7963 90
Mulholland, Rev. A. H. R.	100	0	0	1440	0	0	30	7008 01
Padfield, Rev. James	121	13	4	1378	9	8	52	6678 62
Patterson, Rev. E.	100	0	0	1458	0	0	28	7095 61
Revell, Rev. Henry	121	13	4	1169	4	4	59	5690 19
Salter, Rev. F. G. R.	121	13	4	1636	8	4	39	7962 05
Sandys, Rev. F.	150	0	0	2173	10	0	29	10577 71
Stinson, Rev. E. R.	100	0	0	1440	3	0	30	7008 00
Townley, Rev. A.	121	13	4	1500	16	8	47	7300 73
Ussher, Rev. J. C.	121	13	4	1520	4	0	46	7401 15
Van Linge, Rev. F.	120	0	0	1585	0	0	41	7714 64
Fauquier, Rev. F. D.	100	0	0	1369	0	0	37	6662 47
Street, Rev. ——				1607	4	4	41	7821 79
								$219685 52

* Supplementary Cheque given to make £120.

CHURCH AND STATE IN CANADA. 175

Subsequent to the execution of the powers of attorney given to Mr. Cameron, a bond, supposed to secure to the receiver the provisions of the Imperial and Provincial Acts, was executed by the Church Society and given to the clergy. Here is a copy of the bond :—

"This indenture, made the   day of A.D. 1855, between the Church Society of the Diocese of Toronto, of one part, and A. B., clerk, of the other part. Whereas the said A. B. is a clerk in Holy Orders of the United Church of England and Ireland, and is now the incumbent of the church of   , and, as such incumbent, is now, and has been heretofore, in the receipt of the sum of One Hundred Pounds from the Clergy Reserve Fund; and whereas the said A. B., under and by virtue of a statute lately passed by the Provincial Parliament, is entitled, with the *consent of the Bishop of the said diocese*, to receive from the Government of Canada a certain sum of money, in commutation of his said salary of One Hundred Pounds per annum, and has consented and agreed to pay the said sum, so to be received from the Government as such commutation, to the said Church Society, in consideration of the payment of the said Church Society to the said A. B. of the said sum of One Hundred Pounds per annum, in manner hereafter mentioned, and in further consideration of the several covenants hereinafter mentioned respecting the said commutation money.

"Now, this indenture witnesseth, that for the considerations aforesaid, and in consideration of the said commutation money, *to be paid* by A. B., clerk, to the said Church Society, the said Church Society covenants and agrees with the said A. B., his executors and administrators, that the said Church Society shall and will well and faithfully pay to the said A. B. the annual sum of One Hundred Pounds, by even and equal payments, on the first days of the months of January and July in each and every year, so long as the said A. B. continues to do duty in holy orders as aforesaid in the diocese, and in the event of his being disabled from doing such duty by sickness or bodily or mental infirmity, so long as such sickness or infirmity shall continue; and when and as soon as such annual payment to the said A. B. shall cease, the said Church Society shall have and hold the said commutation money, and all interest and proceeds therefrom upon such trusts, for the *support and maintenance* of the clergy of the said Church within the said diocese, or such other dioceses as the said diocese shall hereafter be divided into, and in such manner as shall from time to time be declared by any by-law or by-laws of the said Church Society, to be from time to time passed for that purpose, so long as the said trusts shall be continued to be administered by the said Society; and in the event of the Synod of the said diocese being legally invested with corporate powers, so as to be enabled to carry out the trusts aforesaid, shall and will transfer and assign the said commutation money, and any securities in which the same may be invested, and all interests and proceeds then unappropriated arising therefrom, to the said Synod, by whatever corporate name called, upon the same trusts, and interests, and purposes, as the same shall and may be held and taken by the said Church Society by virtue of these presents.

"In witness whereof the said Church Society has affixed its corporate seal, and the said A. B. his hand and seal, the day and year first above written.

"In presence of

"C. D."

[L.S.]

[L.S.]

Whatever may have been the effect of the Secularization Act, including this commutation scheme, upon all the religious denominations of the country apart from the Church of England, the question is open as to its freeing the latter from the control of the State; and what kind of control were the clergy of the Church of

CHURCH AND STATE IN CANADA. 179

England subject to? Were they subject to the State or were they subject to the Bishop? Under the bond just quoted, could the Bishop, there being no ecclesiastical discipline or canon in his diocese in force to the contrary, but the reverse—there being a canon authorizing him to issue to any of his clerics permissory or prohibitory documents—give a letter under which a clergyman could suspend active parochial work and yet be entitled to the interest accruing on the capital conveyed by him to the Church Society? Or would it be necessary to apply to and receive permission from a Civil Court?

If the latter alternative were the only one, Church and State are obviously yet in matrimonial relationship. But the first alternative was the only one received and acted upon at the time of the commutation, and it is now in the Diocese of Toronto the only accepted one.

But a more singular inquiry than ever presents itself arising from the two-fold government of Church and State over a donor whose name is given in the list above printed as conveying the sum of $7,008, and who in exchange accepted of the bond just quoted.

Suppose the Bishop gives such an one perpetual leave of absence or a letter of retirement with the express condition that he is to retain "his status on the commutation list"; the letter is made available in good faith—it is never objected to; it is never recalled; it would be puerile for the receiver of the letter, after once accepting of it, to go piteously, without some special reason, and *ask* his diocesan to take it from him and restore him to his former charge, and dispossess the poor curate, or assistant, or successor in the charge; jurisdiction rests between himself and his diocesan—not with another diocese; the trustees of another diocese, holding the capital (both capital and diocese being carved out of the *first*, that is the Diocese of Toronto), seeing an opportunity for litigation, by management bring it on. They cease to pay the claimant. They array their whole hierarchy with its million of dollars, and his own capital too, with their various and vast influences against himself. The plaintiff stands robbed of these advantages, and is without capital.

But the grin does not end here. The trustees, or rather the bishop, the clergy, and lay delegates, in common parlance known as the Synod of the Diocese of Huron, "deny that any sum was received to answer the alleged claim. They do not admit, but deny that the claimant was ever a licensed priest, or that he ever was an incumbent, or recognized in any way as a person entitled to payments out of any funds of the Church." P. 62 Appeal Book. (Signed) S. H. Blake.

S. H. Blake is a brother-in-law of Verschoyle Cronyn, who is the solicitor and chancellor of the Synod; he is also Mr. Cronyn's agent and mouthpiece in litigious proceedings.

As if to intensify the broad grin, the same voice (S. H. B.'s) entered the Toronto assembled Synod and declared that it was "opposed to the starvation principle."

What a travesty upon the commutation scheme as it was termed, and religion itself!

At the moment of refusal to pay, the Bishop (Bethune) who gave the letter of retirement to the claimant died. His solicitor and chancellor, the Hon. John Hillyard Cameron, Q.C., M.P.P., had preceded him to the grave. Bishop Bethune's successor issued from the cradle of litigation and immediately took sides with the hostile trustees and confounded confusion.

However, from the fray the plaintiff rises like the fabled bird, with spotless robes and clean hands, but minus his $7,008; eight years' annuity with interest thereon, in round numbers $3,800; with no provision for the future; $2,800, costs to date, and the voluntary stipend derivable from the parish he held; without a transference to any other diocese in the world, save that which is open to him by virtue of his orders of his last license and letter of retirement.

Hence the singular and never-before-propounded Church and State question as to the responsibility of all the opponents concerned.

Exclamation—What a blending of Church and State, and abnegations of honour as shown in early Christian ethics!

CHAPTER IX.

Accessions of Capital to Diocese of Huron—Agreement with the Clergy—Disputed—Generosity of Clergy Acknowledged—Address to the Hon. John Hillyard Cameron—Popular Suppositions—Speech of Rev. Benjamin Cronyn—Reply of Rev. J. Winterbotham—Speech of Rev. Wm. Ryerson—Centralization—Clerical Visits and Grand Expectations—Exception Taken and Predictions—Influences of Endowments—Truths Circulated in England.

PON the deaths of the Bishop of Toronto (Strachan) and of the Archdeacons of York and Kingston, the further sum of £5,981 6s. 8d. (par value, $29,109.17) passed to the Diocese of Huron, along with other sums of money and many hundreds of acres of land, according to an arrangement entered into by the officials of the Church. And here we have before us a capital, as shown by the commutation list, of $1,113,770.02. Without technicalities being guarded against, the straightforward agreement was, at the time of the commutation, that the individual donors of this large amount should receive the interest at the rate of 6 per cent. per annum accruing thereon during their natural lives. *This* according to the terms of the Imperial and Provincial Acts quoted above. There was to be no rebate or seizure; and should there, by unforeseen casualties, be a deficiency in interest to pay commutants the annual sums they had been accustomed to receive, a draft upon the capital itself should be made equal to the deficiency. It was further thoroughly established in the judgments of the donors that upon their demise their annuity or interest should pass by an equitable division, without equivocation or circuitous manipulation, directly to their successors to be enjoyed by them during *their* natural lives.

The Diocese of Toronto, it appears, has adhered substantially to this rule. But with the

Diocese of Huron varied and vexatious influences have crept in to disturb the application of the funds and to warp the administrative rule. The generation which gave the money has nearly all gone to the grave, and with it the voices of the laity who were familiar with the generosity of the clergy. A new generation of light-hearted clerics, with companions of cheerful laymen, to whom a study of the law and accompanying principles laid down by their fathers proves irksome and unnecessary, has arisen. Among them are to be found a few who assert that the clergy who gave the $1,113,770.02 made a pretence in the bequest, and that the money was never their own to give away. But opposed to this is the circumstance that the Government, under statute made and provided, gave the capital to some non-episcopally ordained gentlemen, who made a personal appropriation of it.

Here is an account of the manner in which the generosity of the clergy was acknowledged. At the first opportunity in Synod assembled, after the $1,113,770.02 was obtained from the clergy, it was resolved :

"That the Lay Delegates embrace this opportunity *unanimously* of informing the clergy with what admiration and gratitude they have witnessed their unbounded liberality and devotion to the cause of religion by surrendering to the Church the commutation money *lately received by them* from the Government, and to assure them that they, on their part, will endeavour to spread abroad among the people the desire of imitating so high an example." (*Canons Diocese of Toronto.*)

During the same session a highly complimentary address was presented to the Hon. John Hillyard Cameron for his unwearied efforts to bring the commutation scheme to a successful issue. Subsequently the Bishop, in an address, put on record: "In the meantime, the commutation was arranged and completed, to which the clergy, to their lasting honour, had given their free and intelligent consent. By this noble and disinterested act they have merited the gratitude of the Church in Canada, and won for themselves the cordial admiration of all true Churchmen throughout the world."

It is popularly supposed that the Secularization Act and subsequent adjustment of the Reserve funds removed all the political influences and personal sources of discomfort and asperity in the Canadian community, and which hitherto distorted the happiness of the people and the material prosperity of the country. But the supposition is fallacious, as experience shows. And instances may be cited where non-endowment advocates not only at the time took exception to what was transpiring, but saw what was likely to occur in the future.

The Rev. Benjamin Cronyn said on the 17th July, 1851, when contending for the holding of land for Church purposes, that "it did not send him into a man's vineyard to steal his grapes, or a man's farmyard to milk his cows."

The Rev. J. Winterbotham replied to this assertion, by saying: "The powers of the Imperial and Provincial Parliaments will necessarily be put forth in relation to this valuable property, because a certain portion of it is now used and dealt with in a manner which is not consistent with the principles of public justice and of general equity. I refer now to my brother from London (meaning the late Bishop Cronyn), who managed to get an Act passed through the Provincial Parliament for the sale of his glebe there. I ask him whether $2,500 was not realized by the sale of that glebe? When a transaction of this nature is seen to take place openly—when public property (according to the views I hold of public property) is thus made a matter of speculative sale, to feed the grasping avarice of those who claim credit for great disinterestedness—I say, when this is the case, it is time for Parliament to interpose."

One more instance, as showing the opinions of those who were bold enough to express them, may be given.

The favourable settlement of 1840 was being referred to, and a claim to still more was being advocated under special appearances of forbearance and amiability of disposition on the part of the special pleaders.

The Rev. Wm. Ryerson was the respondent, and he took occasion to observe that the "courteous rectors appeared to him somewhat like a boa constrictor, after he had gorged a bullock— he is then quite harmless and can be approached without the least danger; but when seeking his prey, under the influence of hunger, he is a most formidable and dangerous creature indeed."

However, the appetite for more in "Huron" does not appear to have been satiated when we read that "Bishop Hellmuth and his clerical assistants collected $102,839" for an educational scheme, and "out of it paid themselves the expenses of collection, $25,602."

Centralization and influence are potential elements in political and ecclesiastical economy; while money has a philosophical screw about it which, like faith, will remove mountains of difficulties, or plunge any institution, with all its adherents, into a Sardonian bog. None should be more familiar with such commonplace truths than the Episcopalian disciples of this western part of our peninsula. For it was from this very part of the Church vineyard that we were instructed for many years prior to the separation of Church and State in the grasping and equivocal assumptions alleged to be practised at Toronto.

Four-horse coaches laden with clerical humanity toiled over tortuous highways stretching between London and Toronto. Clerical Associations were organized and met at accessible parishes as frequently as preparations could be made for the accommodation of guests; and many an intercessory meeting of all the parishioners was held, that the evils of centralizing influences at Toronto, and the accumulations of large sums of money, might be deprecated.

It was also *imprecated*, not deprecated, that if ever a new diocese like that of Huron were organized, family compactism might die and be forever buried in the deeply-dug grave of secularization. And to elevate and preserve a government in the Church equal to a demand for universal respect, and drawing to her fold the allegiance of every one hitherto outside of it, it was predicted that equity would irrigate the gardens of Arimathea as limpid streams flow from pure and never-failing fountains. The technicalities of Shylock bonds, the bleeding expenses of law, and the wranglings of lawyers knew no possibility, even by anticipation— to say nothing of their active pressure—on this side of a common tomb.

Such a universal moral expenditure of funds was to realize to the people, irrespective of class and creed, the advantage of that material support which King George III. and the Imperial Powers sought to confer upon every British subject resident within the limits of this part of Upper Canada. Narrow-minded partizanship, bigotry, and invidious distinctions were to hang as spectres upon a wall that all might see and ask and none reply what their offence had been. *They* were to have none of the sweets of endowment. And so we are left to embrace the announcement that upon the death of the grantors of the $1,113,770.02, the whole becomes subject to the control of the legislative wisdom of every individual member of the community. The spirit and intentions of a grantor are sustained inviolate by his conformity to the jurisdiction of his official superior. A breach of equity or of payment of the stipulated annuity being made by Trustees, Trust Fund Committees, or whatsoever other name they may bear morally and in equity, entitles such grantor to a return to him of the capital placed out of his hands in trust.

Against such an explanation of the manner in which that part of the Clergy Reserve money obtained by the clergy of the Church of England was to be held and distributed we know exception is taken by supporters of State endowments and adherents of the doctrine of Church and State in the present day. And the objection fills every public avenue of opinion with discontent and apprehension. It destroys the cordial support of the laity and admits rancour into places and scenes from which it should be excluded.

The "Voluntaries," as they were termed in times gone by, espied this condition of things;

and it was this very perception which brought together the Rev. Messrs. Winterbotham, Duncan, Gundry, Landon, Pyper, Gilmore, Burns, Roaf, Ryerson, Richardson, Ormiston, Clark and others, to declare with the same voice that the funds of the Church " were exerting and would exert a very dangerous influence upon the opinions of public men in the country ; and that they have been a prolific source of contention and strife in the community from the commencement of their history to the present time." In the same vein, but more vehemently, the principal newspaper of the period also expressed itself.

As far as we have been able we have now redeemed our promise to give a connected rehearsal of the origin and continuation of a substantial desire to make the United Church of England and Ireland the almoner for one-seventh of the territory in the province known as Upper Canada. And evidences of the result are found in a contrast between what the State and " Voluntaries " have accomplished in every city, town, and village where the desire has been encouraged. We have also endeavoured to be impartial and frank in our statements; and as evidences of this we adduce a life and fortune spent in holding up the hands of Mother Church and smoothing the wrinkles in her face.

To attempt to dispossess this Institution of money given to it by one hundred and forty-one clergymen would involve revolutionary measures, no doubt. The evil has grown as an excrescence upon a colony which had a birth, the vigour of youth, and now has attained to manhood. And its very features can only be pleasant or tolerated when men of unbiassed judgments, or of abilities to have a judgment at all, of strict integrity, and educated in soul not less than in *finesse*, constitute the circle of administration. It is an admitted truth that for an individual to be successful, practice and profession must be concurrent.

When newspaper literature began to dawn upon the Old and New World, and had not attained to the celerity with which it can in these times be had, and flashed hourly throughout the uttermost bounds of the universe, there were effective though tardy methods adopted for concentrating it in publishing offices. The old methods, as faithful guides, have been had recourse to in gathering information respecting the kind of *influence* in Huron which " capital " is silently employing over the public mind. And in the face of early culture, interest and position we are driven to the conclusion, and are obliged to submit to it, that such influence is actually filling the prediction made in respect to it years ago;—that it is warping the opinions of public men, promoting litigation, encouraging parochial gossip, holding out food for the insincere and cynical to feed upon and eructate for abusive purposes, and drying up the fountains of a general liberality;—in a word, that it is *not* a beneficent influence and deserves to be removed by some widespread salutary legislative proceedings. All in a very remarkable style involuntarily repeating axioms circulated throughout the length and breadth of England—that no spiritual power can dwell in the midst of a *secular* one ; no *heavenly* kingdom can be established in the very midst of an *earthly* one, unless reason is convinced by a generous administration, judgment swayed by an equitable disposal of financial resources, and a trustful, loving confidence secured for the good of every citizen.

CONCLUSION.

For half a century the Editor of this compilation has taken an active interest in the material and moral prosperity of his native land. He has been too liberal and unsuspecting in pioneer efforts to promote a polity embracing these objects. The grapes he grew in his own vineyard are being eaten by adjusting officials, and episcopal lawn is draggled in the dust or beclouded by an administrative army, having none of the advantages of instruction derivable from a principle of rotation and experience.

The beauty of government consists in simplicity; it appears to be a favourite maxim that there should be no strutting administration between an executive officer and those subject to his control. It also is an admitted maxim in America that executive authority originates with the people. When the first is discarded, the latter is necessarily adopted; and to the people an appeal can be made, no doubt, with the best results, when a victim discloses to them the manner in which he has been dismantled of his rights. At any rate, such has been the voice of experience, and we have confidence in relying upon it now that the heavy hand of injustice grips us with merciless fingers.

But a last view we submit for approval, and it is this: That during the period of our activity and enterprises in this part of Canada many improvements have been introduced by civil authorities and private individuals. Many people and races have arrived who are without information respecting the subject of "Separation," and native generations are attaining to mature years without acquiring a knowledge of the religious political struggles of their predecessors; while the supposed advantages secured for everyone are in danger of lapsing into evils of no common magnitude. Even the tolerably and well educated are found throughout the whole country who speak of their resources with a flippancy, and treat by-gone generosity with an indifference which it is neither pleasant nor profitable to realize. If either or both of these dispositions can be removed by a perusal of the preceding pages, and a sedate inquiry awakened in the minds of a progressive people in respect to the result of a Separation of the Church from the State, we conceive that a benefit will follow and attach to this compilation. We speak of the *Separation* in its popular acceptation. For a *complete* Separation has not occurred, otherwise we would not witness the wrangling of lawyers over denominational and religious differences of opinion, nor find courts adjudicating over some millions of dollars held in trust for the promotion of the tenets of a particular Church, established, so far as this very money is concerned, upon this peninsular part of the Dominion.

A popular mistake, it is assumed, has still further been received and acted upon by the public, from a supposition that the $1,113,770, given first by the Government to individuals by way of dispensing with their services as a State paid clergy, and then by them to an open Society, *have not been* so donated for the aid and comfort of every soul constituting the public. When, as a matter of principle and of right, every one having ears to hear, a voice or a judgment to receive and be influenced by knowledge, is as much entitled to advantages (if there are any at all) accruing from what is recognized as "commutation money," as the three or four who may manipulate the whole.

During the past summer at Montreal by the Provincial Synod, the union of all denominations was trenchantly canvassed, and if this action did not involve and advocate the principle of admitting the public to representation touching Commutation Trust Funds instead of to a circle of catechised adherents, then we know not what constitutes an affirmation. At all events, no provision was made by commutants against the introduction of a voice from all races and creeds for the expenditure of their capital or for the exclusion of legislative enactments, co-extensive in their application with other laws of the land. The present system of administering the Clergy Reserve money is limited, and encourages centralization. It leads along ambitious paths for party purposes in religion, and when prejudices are awakened the innocent are made to suffer. The period of age anticipated and provided for by the Imperial and Provincial Governments, and supposed to be secured to each one who received and gave a specified sum at the time of a general disposal of the Reserve Funds, has been discovered to be, after thirty-three years of adoption, eight years of deprivation, and as many in equivocal chancery, wholly a futile arrangement; that a combination of men may be brought to the front, who, veiled by a construction of law not always in accord with justice, may thwart the very best of designs and send down to the grave in penury, with all its miserable companions, the subjects of their disregard.

The spirit of every writer whom we quote appears to be confirmatory of this remark, and the conclusion is that State Endowment adherents are now, as formerly, "behind the age."

However, we do not presume to originate opinions, and it is left for every reader to advocate or disallow according to the instruction he has had and the judgment resulting from it.

www.ingramcontent.com/pod-product-compliance
Lightning Source LLC
Chambersburg PA
CBHW020919230426
43666CB00008B/1503